Endangered Gospel

Endangered Gospel

How Fixing the World is Killing the Church

JOHN C. NUGENT

 CASCADE *Books* · Eugene, Oregon

ENDANGERED GOSPEL
How Fixing the World is Killing the Church

Cascade Books
An Imprint of Wipf and Stock Publishers
199 W. 8th Ave., Suite 3
Eugene, OR 97401

www.wipfandstock.com

PAPERBACK ISBN: 978-1-4982-9166-8
HARDCOVER ISBN: 978-1-4982-9168-2
EBOOK ISBN: 978-1-4982-9167-5

Cataloguing-in-Publication data:

Names: Nugent, John C.
Title: Endangered gospel : how fixing the world is killing the church / John C. Nugent.
Description: Eugene, OR: Cascade Books, 2016 | Includes bibliographical references and indexes.
Identifiers: ISBN 978-1-4982-9166-8 (paperback) | ISBN 978-1-4982-9168-2 (hardcover) | ISBN 978-1-4982-9167-5 (ebook)
Subjects: LCSH: 1. Church. | 2. Eschatology. | 3. Discipleship. | 4. Missions. | I. Title.
Classification: BV598 .N7 2016 (print) | BV598 (ebook)

Manufactured in the U.S.A.   JUNE 11, 2016

Dedicated To
Delta Community Christian Church
for striving to be God's better place in this world

Contents

Acknowledgments

ENDANGERED GOSPEL IS NOT the book I sat down to write. I had planned to write a shorter and simpler book about the priestly witness of God's people. In fact, I had that book almost entirely mapped out. But each time I set my pen to paper, bits and pieces of this book came out instead. I am quite certain that Delta Community Christian Church is mostly to blame.

Near the beginning of this project, I was preparing to preach at our annual church retreat. During that process, I couldn't shake the feeling that what God gave me to share with my church family was more pressing than what I originally planned to share with you. What I shared with them was a combination of what they had been teaching me in our life together and what I had been learning from the Scriptures.

That retreat had a profound impact on me. What I presented about the gospel and its meaning for the church resonated deeply with the wider body. Many in our church look back at those conversations as a game changer in our faith journey and life together. Their honest questions and enthusiastic affirmations confirmed that *this* is the book I needed to write. Indeed, I couldn't have written it without them.

Similar encouragement came from my students at Great Lakes Christian College and my good friends at the Outhouse Ministers Retreat. It is a blessing to kick ideas around with both young students whose imaginations are less constrained by "the real world" *and* devoted ministers who labor day in and day out to keep "the real world" from swallowing up their congregations. Their combined idealism and experience have made this a much stronger book.

I am also grateful to people like John Gleason who have devoted considerable time to reading drafts of this book and engaging me in thoughtful conversation. Some of my readers have gone even further and have given detailed advice as to how my content and writing may be improved. I am humbled by the countless hours that such friends have devoted to this project, including Branson Parler, Ted Troxell, Kate Blakely, Jordan Kellicut, Jordan Ickes, Margaryta Teslina, Dale Burgess, Ryan Apple, Joel Ickes, and Aaron Woods. Aaron also supplied most of the clarifying questions that I engage in the appendix.

Finally, I am privileged to thank my wife, Beth, as well as our three girls—Alissa, Sierra, and Alexia. Being an active church member, teacher, and writer means devoting a lot of time to people and projects. I am blessed with loving family members who partner with me in these endeavors to such an extent that they are a part of our shared life, rather than a drain on "family life."

Thank you, God, for giving such good gifts to your children.

Part One:

The Case for a Better Place

1

Yearning for a Better Place

Endangered Species

I FIRST VISITED SEA World in junior high. My experience was mixed: I was amazed by the creatures, but bothered by all the preaching. Everywhere I went, someone was lobbying to preserve some nearly extinct animal. It was Spring Break; I didn't want to sit through lectures about endangered species—however adorable manatees may be. I was there for thrilling rides and exotic sights. Show me the sharks!

I've come a long way since junior high, and so have the manatees. Thanks to the Endangered Species Act and numerous other initiatives, the population of these docile sea cows has increased 500 percent since 1991. As of January 2016, they are scheduled to be downgraded from "endangered" to "threatened."[1] This is what happens when people of good will join together and mobilize for a common cause.

But marine mammals may be the least of our problems. The wider world is in considerable danger. Wars rage among volatile countries. Terrorists strike unsuspecting cities. Mass shootings frequent the most developed countries. Poverty is a global phenomenon, gendercide still plagues Eastern regions, and pollutants contaminate major water supplies. This world remains a dangerous place. But is it so endangered that Christians must mobilize to protect it?

1. Grinberg and Couwels, "Manatees Set for Removal from U.S. Endangered Species List."

Christian Activism

Christians have long acknowledged that this world is broken. To us this is old news. Sin has been wreaking havoc on this world since the garden of Eden. What is new is how eager Christians are to do something about it. In the past, we've wanted to save people *from* this broken world. Nowadays, we want to fix it. We want to end war, purify water, feed the poor, and eradicate all forms of discrimination. We don't just want to talk about it; we want to do something and make a difference.

This Christian desire to "do something" goes way back. Second-century Christians did something by rescuing abandoned babies from Roman gutters. Medieval men and women took vows of poverty and chastity to better serve the poor. Fearless Christians harbored Jews who were fleeing from Hitler's soldiers.

Since the early twentieth century, liberal Christians have been working hard to make this world a better place. Meanwhile, evangelical believers debated whether the church should pursue social justice or just stick to saving souls. That debate is mostly over: God cares about both, and so should we.

I agree that Christians should do something. God has indeed called his people to do something. But I wonder, has God really called us to fix the world? Is this what Jesus meant by calling us salt and light? Are we even capable of fixing this world? Is it something that God has empowered us to do?

We May Not Be Able to Change the World

James Davison Hunter has written an insightful book about changing the world.[2] Hunter is a devout Christian who believes that the church has a vital role to play. He is also an astute sociologist who examines history, observes trends, and identifies the causes and effects of world change.

Many people believe that big changes happen when ordinary individuals stand for what is right. They roll up their sleeves, enter the fray, and fix whatever ails society around them. This is how pop culture likes to portray what turns the tide of world history. The "movers" and "shakers" are heroic and humble people who do something.

2. Hunter, *To Change the World*, 1–47.

Hunter disagrees. That's not how the world really changes, he argues. Culture changes from the top down, not the bottom up. Though bottom-up movements achieve specific goals, their achievements are often short-lived and limited in scope. Exceptional individuals accomplish great good on a local scale and positively impact the lives of hundreds, even thousands of people. But lasting change happens, Hunter argues, when elite persons who are close to the center of social power rally the masses around a movement that is already growing in momentum. Though such movements draw from the frustration and activism of grassroots folk, they take off only after elite leaders champion their causes.

Hunter further explains that the ability to shape culture is concentrated in elite institutions with a monopoly on the tools of cultural manipulation. Even powerful elites cannot change the world by themselves. They need to be connected to overlapping networks of social, cultural, economic, and political influence. When such networks join together with a common purpose, they can and do bring sweeping change.

Just ask the manatees. These vulnerable mammals found protection under a series of federal and state laws, with violators facing stiff fines and possible imprisonment. The Marine Mammal Protection Act took effect in 1972, the Endangered Species Act kicked in a year later, and the Florida Manatee Sanctuary Act followed in 1978. The U.S. Fish & Wildlife Service then began coordinating the Florida Manatee Recovery Plan in 1980. Nearly a decade later, Florida's Governor and Cabinet directed their state wildlife agency to pressure specific counties to reduce manatee injury and death.[3]

Yet lasting change required more than political persuasion. So performing artist Jimmy Buffet partnered with Senator Bob Graham to launch the Save the Manatee Club in 1981.[4] Wealthy philanthropists were encouraged to support this cause. Others could also sponsor a manatee with modest contributions. Meanwhile, high-profile theme parks rallied behind them with impassioned pleas looping repeatedly over loudspeakers to raise awareness among countless patrons waiting in park lines. Only a multipronged, coordinated effort of this magnitude could get the job done—and, decades later, it did.

3. http://www.savethemanatee.org/manfcts.htm.
4. http://www.savethemanatee.org.

Whether we like it or not, Hunter seems to be right. Changing the world takes complex networks of elite people in strategic places with abundant resources.

But What about the Bible?

If you are like me, you are probably thinking that Hunter's top-down, power-politicking explanation doesn't sound biblical. What about Jesus' mustard seed teaching? Didn't God call Abraham away from the power center of Babylon in order to make him a great nation? Didn't God bring the Israelites out of the cultural epicenter of Egypt to continue that work? Didn't Jesus mostly ignore the important political players in the Roman world of his day? Didn't he pick a ragtag bunch of bumbling Galileans to represent his cause?

The God of Scripture seems to be anything but elitist. On only the rarest of occasions do we find his people hobnobbing among the highbrow. Even then, it was under duress and not by choice.

- Joseph was sold into slavery and dragged into prison before rising to prominence in Egypt (Gen 37–40).

- Moses was sent away by his mother in order to escape infanticide before ending up in Pharaoh's house (Exod 1–2).

- Daniel and his friends were captured and taken into exile before finding themselves in the Babylonian court where they were hardly paragons of cooperation (Dan 1–6).

- Esther was forced into a demeaning beauty pageant and felt pressured to conceal her identity before eventually becoming queen of Persia (Esth 2).

None of these figures engineered their own rise to power so they would be strategically positioned to fix the world. Rather, God used their unfortunate circumstances to preserve the posterity of his endangered people.

- Joseph spared the offspring of Abraham from a deadly famine in Canaan (Gen 42:1–2).

- Moses saved his kin from extinction in Egypt (Exod 1:8–22).

- Daniel foiled imperial edicts that would have driven God's people to compromise or extermination (Dan 3:6; 6:7).

- Esther overturned an edict authorizing Jewish genocide (Esth 3:5–15).

The methods Hunter identifies as essential for world change simply don't square well with Scripture. It wasn't the way of Israel, and it certainly wasn't the way of Jesus and his followers.

If Hunter is right about what it takes to change the world, and we're right about what the Bible says about the call of God's people, then perhaps the God of Scripture hasn't called his people to make this world a better place. If God hasn't asked us to fix this world, then many well-intentioned Christians are misappropriating time, energy, and resources that God has given us for other purposes.

If we're not careful, we may gain the world and lose the church—and then, ultimately, we'll lose the world, too. When Christians begin substituting activism for discipleship, it's not the world that becomes endangered, but the gospel.

2

Incomplete Visions of a Better Place

LET ME BE AS straightforward and clear as possible: it's not the church's job to make this world a better place.

Don't get me wrong. I, too, want this world to be better. I want it as much as anyone else. I hope my three daughters and future grandchildren grow up in the best possible world. Yet my desire—however strong and pure it may be—does not trump God's word. Were we to do what it takes to make this world better, we may ultimately fail to do the very thing God has called us to do in Scripture.

I know this doesn't sound very responsible. What is worse, it sounds downright lazy or apathetic. It conjures up hackneyed images of pious people leaning back in their easy chairs or clasping hands in holy huddles singing pious platitudes while this world goes to hell in a handbasket.

There are people who think that withdrawing—that letting go and letting God—is the way Christians should act. I'm not one of those people. What God has actually called his people to do is far more demanding of our time, energy, and resources than most card-carrying agents of world betterment dare to imagine. It's also far more in line with this world's best interests. This book is not about retreating from the world, but engaging the world in the best possible way—the way that only we can.

The church has approached the concept of a better place in many different ways. It is helpful to identify those ways and to discuss their similarities and differences. I have classified them into four types: heaven centered, human centered, world centered, and kingdom centered. In this chapter I discuss the first three types, each of which falls short for various reasons. In chapter 3, I introduce the kingdom-centered type.

The remainder of the book is dedicated to making the case for and exploring the implications of this fourth type.

The Heaven-Centered View: Go to a Better Place

For almost two millennia, most Christians have hoped to leave behind all the pain of bodily existence in a fallen world and go to heaven after they die. Such people are realistic about sin's destructive consequences and skeptical that much good will come from the mess that sin has made of God's good creation. So God sent Jesus to provide a way out.

Some people believe this happens immediately after we die. Others associate it with the second coming of Jesus. Either way, their conviction is that Jesus will raise his people from the dust of the earth and take them to be where he has been since ascending to heaven to prepare a better place for them.

According to this view, God's kingdom is *not here* and *not yet*. It is in the future and in heaven. Proponents of this view seldom claim to know exactly what life in heaven will be like, but it will most certainly be a better place that is free from sin's negative consequences. So the primary role of the church is to spread the word about how Jesus paved the way to a better place. After convincing people that Jesus is the way, the church's role is to make sure they will be found acceptable on judgment day. When heaven is the better place, earth is a bad or at least worse place, and the church functions as a recruiting and holding place.

This view has fallen on hard times for many reasons. For starters, views of heaven have changed dramatically since the rise of modern science. Heaven was once believed to be the realm of God's abode just beyond the clouds, but out of sight from the naked human eye. Now that the Hubble Space Telescope and its successors can see deeply into outer space, it is quite clear that the universe is much more immense than we ever imagined. Most people now agree that God's abode must be a realm altogether different from the space-time continuum we now inhabit.

This has led many to conclude that this world is all that God ever intended for humans. It has also driven them back to the Bible to discern what exactly it says about heaven and earth. What they have found comes as a surprise to many. Scripture never directly says that people go to heaven after they die.[1] At most, one might infer that human souls are stored there temporarily until judgment day.

1. See Middleton, *A New Heaven and a New Earth*; Snyder, *Salvation Means*

Instead, heaven is described as the realm of God and his angels, and earth is depicted as the realm of humans. In Scripture, resurrection means a return to life on this earth, albeit an earth that God will renew and make a much better place. I discuss the earthly location of God's kingdom in greater depth in chapter 9.

The bottom line is that the kingdom of heaven is not a place *in heaven*. It is a reality in which God's will is done *"on earth* as it is in heaven" (Matt 6:10). Though most believers and a good number of unbelievers once adhered to the heaven-centered view, it is rapidly losing ground—so much so that it is no more likely to make a comeback than flat earth or geocentric universe theories.

The Human-Centered View: Make this World a Better Place

Believers who abandon all hope of someday going to heaven typically embrace an earth-oriented view. The one we consider here has much in common with non-Christian views of this world. Since many unbelievers see life in this world as all that will ever be, the noblest way to live is to strive to make this world a better place.

The Christian version of this view goes further.[2] It affirms that when Jesus came and preached the kingdom of God, he was establishing a charter for how God's will could be done on earth as in heaven. He was casting a world-transforming vision of social and economic justice. When people of faith embrace this vision and put it into action, they advance God's kingdom and make this world better. Jesus began making this world a better place. It is the church's responsibility to finish the job.

I call this view "human centered" because it is pretty much up to humans to make this world a better place. In Jesus, God revealed what needs to be done, but it is up to us to do it. God is not going to intervene and set things right. Things will progressively improve only as humans embrace and implement God's vision on a global scale.

Proponents of this view differ as to whether this vision will ever fully become a reality. For some, the kingdom is an impossible ideal that serves to keep us reaching in the right direction. For others, it will be reached in the fullness of time. With God's help, humans will step it up and build a better future.

Creation Healed; and Wright, *Surprised by Hope.*

2. Walter Rauschenbusch famously represented this position, which is often called the social gospel, in *A Theology for the Social Gospel.*

There are different ways people work out the details of what happens next. The most important and central idea is this: history progresses in stages toward the kingdom of God through human effort. We should not expect a dramatic divine intervention, but slow and steady movement in the right direction.

The strongest criticism of this view is its optimistic take on what humans can and will accomplish in this world. It was more popular in the late nineteenth and early twentieth century, before the northern hemisphere was ripped apart by two world wars. Advances in medicine, technology, and education made it seem as if this world were indeed getting progressively better. It was well on its way to God's kingdom vision.

Since then, however, it has been one terrible war after another. Age-old battles are still being fought, and the recent explosion in global communication has multiplied human awareness of how sick and distorted this world remains. The same technology that increases our ability to extend human life also increases our ability to destroy one another and God's good creation.

Meanwhile, Christians continue to see their influence decline in parts of the world they once controlled. It has become increasingly difficult to imagine this world getting significantly better without some sort of dramatic divine intervention.

The World-Centered View: Work Toward Making this World the Better Place to Come

The fastest growing Christian view of a better place is world centered. It is most critical of the heaven-centered view. In keeping with the spirit of our age, its proponents tend to be ecologically sensitive. God made this world, he cares about this world, his people should care about this world, and he will indeed redeem this world.

Their case is deeply rooted in Scripture. They highlight multiple passages in both testaments that imply a central role of nonhuman creation in God's redemptive work.[3] And they reject the patchwork of verses that must be taken out of context to support a vision of hope that leaves this earth behind and transports God's people to heaven for eternal bliss.[4]

3. Isa 2:2–4, 11:1–16, 30:18–26, 35:1–10, 65:17–25; Mic 4:1–4; Ezek 40–48; Acts 3:21; Rom 8:19–23; Eph 1:10; Col 1:19–20; Rev 21:1—22:7.

4. Matt 5:12, 6:20, 7:21; Luke 16:19–26, 23:43; John 14:2–3; 2 Cor 5:1, 12:2; Phil 1:20–24, 3:14; Col 1:5; 1 Thess 4:13–18; 2 Tim 4:18; Heb 3:1; 1 Pet 1:4.

Here is not the place to describe all of their arguments, but it is worth noting that the world-centered view enjoys widespread support from Bible scholars all over the theological spectrum.[5]

Though humans play an important role in this view, it holds forth little hope that we will ever bring God's kingdom. Human progress in history does not accumulate in such a way that this world becomes better and better.

The heaven-centered view is right that if we are ever to inhabit a significantly better world, God himself will have to make it so. Yet God is going to remake *this world* into a better place and not whisk us away to another one. Only this kind of divine intervention, according to the world-centered view, truly fulfills the earthly hopes of Scripture, and only a future bodily resurrection enables all God's saints to enjoy it.

The world-centered view's insistence on a robust future hope doesn't detract from its conviction that the renewed world for which we wait has already in a real sense begun with Jesus. When Jesus came the first time, he didn't just announce a future better place. In his life, death, and resurrection, he started making *this world* a better place. In Christ, all things are new. Creation is already being freed from bondage. The new world to come is already under way.

If God's kingdom began to break into the old order when Jesus came and he will complete it when he returns, then where do God's people fit in? What is left for the church to do? Though this view believes humans cannot make this world the better place God intends it to be, it still holds God's people responsible for doing the best we can. Since God is in the business of world betterment, we ought to join him in it. We must denounce injustice wherever we encounter it and work to transform wider society in the direction of God's kingdom.

In so doing, according to this view, we reclaim our original role as God's royal image bearers. When God created humans in his image, he gave us dominion over creation (Gen 1:26–28). We were placed in charge and commissioned to look after creation on God's behalf. We were supposed to create healthy cultures in which all God's creatures could thrive and live together in harmony. But we failed at this task. We embraced a life of sin, corrupted our reflection of God's image, and distorted our dominion mandate.

---

5. See, for example, Middleton's *A New Heaven and a New Earth*, Snyder's *Salvation Means Creation Healed*, and Wright's, *Surprised by Hope*.

But, the view continues, Christ changed all of this. He inaugurated a new creation in which God's people might reclaim our rightful role as his image bearers. We may now exercise dominion the way we were supposed to from the very beginning. So we should avoid the false choice between *thinking* we can fix this world (since we can't) and *abstaining* from even trying (since we won't). Rather we will bring God's future world into the present wherever and whenever possible. Though we cannot redeem this world, none of our world-redeeming labors will go to waste; they point to, participate in, and will be folded into God's ultimate global redemption.

Of course, the church's work is not limited to world betterment. God's people must first order their own house according to the kingdom. Our life together should be a sign and a foretaste of God's new creation. It is the place where God's new world is most visible in the here and now. If we cannot order our own lives according to God's kingdom, we have no business telling others how to reorder theirs. Our newness of life together serves as our credentials for pursuing world betterment in wider society with integrity.

BETTER PLACE TYPOLOGY I

	Salvation in Heaven	Salvation on Earth	Restoration began with Jesus	Future interruption	God replaces fallen order	Christians begin fixing fallen order
Heaven Centered	X			X	X	
Human Centered		X				X
World Centered		X	X	X		X

As this chart illustrates, the world-centered view appears to have struck the perfect balance between the first two views we considered. With the heaven-centered view, it shares high hopes for a future divine intervention, while rejecting an excessively low view of earthly creation and emphasizing that God's restoration of this world has already begun. With the human-centered view, it shares a strong desire to make this world a better place, while rejecting unwarranted optimism that humans might actually pull it off.

It is little wonder, then, that the world-centered approach is fast becoming the new favorite. Though it is a considerable upgrade over the other views, it remains a work in progress. It, too, has shortcomings that need to be addressed. Clearing them out of the way will enable us to see a better way forward.

3

Toward a Better Vision of a Better Place

Shortcomings of the World-Centered View

LET ME BEGIN BY saying that the world-centered view is clearly the best option presented so far. It is right on target in four ways:

- It focuses on this world.
- It denies that humans will bring the kingdom.
- It acknowledges that the kingdom has already begun in Jesus.
- It insists that Jesus will return to finalize God's kingdom and raise the faithfully departed to enjoy that kingdom forever.

What I find lacking is its ecclesiology—how it presents the church's nature and mission. Though it recognizes the uniqueness of God's set-apart people, it does not properly distinguish between the specific calling of God's people and the generic calling of all people. It presumes that because God will ultimately restore all things, it is the church's job to begin restoring all things. Though we will not bring God's kingdom, we are still responsible for striving to make the world a better place.

It's as if Jesus came and made a huge splash in world history only to leave behind a people whose role is to announce this splash and then try to do a better job than their unbelieving neighbors at fixing the old creation. On the ground, its social agenda is hardly distinguishable from middle class do-goodism and run-of-the-mill humanitarianism. In an effort to recapture a biblical vision of global restoration, it has infused world management into the church's mission in ways that are alien to the New Testament.

We must reckon with the fact that Jesus never tells his followers to roll up their sleeves, enter the fray of broken pagan societies, denounce their wrongful ways, and help them get on the right track with the gospel message they received from him. Nor do the apostolic letters ever reprimand the earliest believers for not taking more initiative to clean up Roman streets, protest unjust laws, or launch social programs that ease the financial burden of the poorest members of society.

Though it may seem embarrassing, Jesus, Paul, Peter, James, Jude, and John paid little attention to making the wider world a better place. It only gets worse when one scrolls back through the Old Testament. The laws of Moses never instruct the Israelites to use their God-given way of life to improve the lot of people beyond their own borders. The prophets—who held nothing back when criticizing God's people—never condemn the Israelites for neglecting poor and needy neighbors who lived outside their land, even those in smaller and weaker nearby nations like Edom, Ammon, and Moab.

Yet the world-centered vision derives its world-betterment calling from somewhere. Its proponents often support it with common misreadings of Scripture, which are not unique to them.

- They turn the prophets' condemnation of Israelite-to-Israelite social injustices into a license to denounce and overturn all injustices everywhere (Amos 2:6–8).

- They expand songs from Mary and Zechariah about God's exaltation of lowly Israelites into promises that God will liberate all oppressed groups (Luke 1:46–56, 68–79).

- They make instruction from Jesus and James about caring for needy fellow believers into a universal decree to end global poverty (Luke 18:22; Jas 1:27).

- They stretch generic statements about the unique ruling responsibility of humankind into a specific mandate for God's people (Gen 1:26).

- They misapply forward-looking statements about the royal role of God's people in the new heavens and earth to the church's mission before Christ's return (Rev 5:10).

I will return to these misreadings later. For now, it is important to address a more fundamental problem, which is the failure of this view to properly distinguish between three different aspects of creation:

- Nonhuman creation (planet earth, soil, seas, sky, animals).
- The new human order made possible by Christ (the church).
- Old human orders of creation (governing structures, economic systems, public service agencies).

In Scripture, these created aspects are distinct, though they have certain things in common (displayed in the chart below). All three suffer corruption due to sin. The church and nonhuman creation will be perfected when Christ returns. The old human orders are passing away and will eventually be eliminated. And only the new human order made possible by Christ participates *already* in God's ultimate project of renewal. There is thus a significant distinction between what is happening *now* among God's people and what is happening *now* in and throughout the wider world.

	Suffer Corruption	Will be Perfected	Will be Eliminated	Now Being Renewed
Nonhuman Creation	X	X		
New Human Order in Christ	X	X		X
Old Human Orders	X		X	

This distinction is important for many reasons. For one, God is doing a revolutionary thing *now* among his people, but *not yet* in the wider world. We may not like that, but God is the one who gets to choose when things get done, and God knows what is best. If Christians prioritize the world at the church's expense, they are actually getting in God's way, which is ultimately bad for the world.

There is certainly a place for humans to care about nonhuman creation, and the world will certainly be better off for it. I discuss this in Part Three. But failure to prioritize the new human order made possible by Christ means failure to do for nonhuman creation and the old human order the specific thing that we have been called to do and that no one besides us can do. What is worse, it is possible for the revolutionary thing God is doing among his people to be domesticated and made servant to various projects of wider world betterment to which God has not called his people.

The distinction that the New Testament makes between nonhuman creation and the new human order in Christ is made clear in Romans:

> For the creation waits with eager longing for the revealing of the children of God; for the creation was subjected to futility, not of its own will but by the will of the one who subjected it, in hope that the creation itself will be set free from its bondage to decay and will obtain the freedom of the glory of the children of God. We know that the whole creation has been groaning in labor pains until now; and not only the creation, but we ourselves, who have the first fruits of the Spirit, groan inwardly while we wait for adoption, the redemption of our bodies. (8:20–23)[1]

Verse 20 is key because it depicts creation itself as longing for divine intervention. Yet the intervention for which it longs is not the restoration of the old fallen order. Rather, it anticipates the day when God's children will be revealed for what we truly are: the forerunners and champions of God's new order. Creation knows that God's children are the true movers and shakers of world history. We are world history's future. We uniquely possess the first fruits of the Spirit—the Spirit of the world to come. Our renewal has already begun, though we await the redemption of our bodies when Christ returns.

Creation has not yet begun to experience its restoration, except perhaps secondhand through God's people. Whenever the Apostle Paul uses "new creation" language, he is talking about the new social reality of God's people (Gal 6:15) and the new way we perceive and interact with all of creation (2 Cor 5:16–20). Yet the rocks, trees, and fields still groan for their restoration to begin. They eagerly long for a future that is not tied to the betterment of the old human orders that currently manage the world. Rather, they look forward to riding the coattails of God's children whose life together already bustles with newness of life in God's kingdom.

My point is this: the world-centered approach risks putting the cart before the horse. Even though the New Testament presumes and proclaims God's redemption, reconciliation, and restoration of all things, it gives primacy to the new thing that has already begun among God's people. What Christ has begun to do *in the church* is the core of what will be folded into his ultimate renovation of all things. The order of priority is first Christ, then his renewed people, and finally the redemption of our bodies and of nonhuman creation.

---

1. Unless indicated otherwise, all Scripture quotations are from the NRSV.

A Better Way Forward

To make the case for a better vision, I must do more than highlight the weaknesses of competing views. I need to showcase the superior strength of the vision I am casting. At this point, it is tempting to rush to the conclusion and set forth a more biblical view in its entirety. Though that might be helpful, I want the alternative to rise up from within the Bible story told well. This will be the focus of Part Two. After walking through the Bible story together, with a keen eye on the place of God's people, we will be prepared to complete the typology I began above and discuss its implications for the church today.

A better way forward will begin with two fundamental truths:

- Jesus has already made a better place in this world.

- The role of God's people is to embrace, display, and proclaim this better place.

These truths may seem too simplistic. Of course Jesus made things better in this world. Of course we need to reflect that. Doesn't everyone believe that already?

Yes. Most believers would affirm these statements. But they often combine them with a few truths that confuse the church's self-understanding and mission. They might say something like, "Because Jesus began making a better place in this world, we must join him in seeing it through to completion, until the whole world is better." Or, "We should certainly embrace and convey the better place that Christ makes possible. And we should also do everything in our power to shape the wider society accordingly."

These additional truths suppose that Jesus sowed the seeds of world betterment and our job is to water and help them grow. They are wrong.

It might be helpful to state these two fundamental truths in a different way:

- Since Jesus has already made a better place in this world, it is *not* our responsibility to do so.

- Since our job is to embrace, display, and proclaim this better place, it is *not* our job to engineer or otherwise orchestrate its fulfillment.

Put simply, *God's people are not responsible for making this world a better place. They are called to be the better place that Christ has already made and that the wider world will not be until Christ returns.*

God's people are not called, in Scripture, to enter all spheres of life and straighten them out to make this world better. God calls his people to a specific way of life. That way of life participates in and invites all people to the new and better world that God has already begun in Christ.

This book is not another attempt to promote countercultural Christianity. I am not encouraging Christians to step up their witness *against* this fallen world. God has set his people apart from the world precisely so we can serve the fallen world in ways that only we can. We Christians need to enter more fully into the new world order made possible by Christ. Only this will enable us to offer the true service that God has asked us to render on his behalf.

Striving to make this world a better place oversteps the bounds of our mission, eclipses part of the gospel, and leads us to neglect our true calling. It is in this sense that the gospel is "endangered." It is not that God can't or won't finish his work of salvation if our generation confuses the good news and neglects our primary responsibility. Like Mordecai told Esther, should she pass on her opportunity to save God's people, relief and deliverance would come from somewhere else (Esth 4:14). God's promises will not fail and his plans will come to fruition. But if we want to be an integral part of them, we must embrace the specific opportunity he has given us.

Part Two: The Bible's Story of a Better Place

Well-meaning believers justify out-of-bounds actions because they place undue emphasis upon obscure biblical passages. They largely ignore key themes that span Scripture and lead to different conclusions. I make these themes visible in Part Two of this book by telling the biblical story of a better place in ten stages:

1. God Creates a Very Good Place

2. Humans Corrupt God's Very Good Place

3. God Uses the Powers to Make this World a Better Place

4. God Forms a People to Prepare for a Better Place

5. God Sends Jesus to Inaugurate a Better Place, Part I

6. God Sends Jesus to Inaugurate a Better Place, Part II

7. God Calls the Church to Embrace a Better Place

8. God Calls the Church to Display a Better Place

9. God Calls the Church to Proclaim a Better Place

10. God Makes this World the Very Best Place

By the time you are done reading stage three, it will be clear why Christians need a better vision of a better place. When you are finished with stage ten, the nature of that better place will be clear as well as the precise role of God's people within it. Then it will be time to revisit and complete the Better Place Typology chart.

Returning to the Bible story is vitally important. Christians routinely confuse their calling because they are biblically illiterate. Or, what is sometimes worse, they think they know the story, but they are only familiar with dwarf tellings that leave out key components that are necessary for getting our story straight.

The telling I offer in Part Two sketches the Old Testament backgrounds, centers on the work of Christ, and makes crystal clear the role of the church.

Part Three: A Better Place in Action

Part Three discusses the practical implications of the biblical vision set forth in Part Two. We will explore its implications for discipleship, leadership, fellowship, family relationships, friendship, vocation, missions, and witness to the powers.

In many ways, Part Three is the most important part of the book. It both applies the better view I am offering to Christians today and it answers some common objections. For example, many Christians feel called to participate in specific humanitarian activities. Part Three shows how such activities are secondary to Christian mission, yet still important as accent pieces to God's central work.

This is important for a generation of activists because faithfulness is not simply a matter of doing the right things with pure motives. It is also about not doing the wrong things, and putting the right things in their proper place. It means keeping central things in the center and peripheral things on the periphery. It means not making a career out of a corrective.

Jesus' problem with the scribes and Pharisees was not that they taught the wrong things. Rather, they lived the wrong way because their priorities were off-kilter. The Sadducees and Zealots of Jesus' day were also eager for God's kingdom. Yet, because they did not seek it in God's way, they often found themselves on the wrong side of God's will.[2]

Contemporary Christian activists are right. It is time for God's people to do something. But let's be sure to do the right thing. Jesus said to some of the do-something activists of his day,

> Not everyone who says to me, "Lord, Lord," will enter the king-
> dom of heaven, but only the one who does the will of my Father
> in heaven. On that day many will say to me, "Lord, Lord, did we
> not prophesy in your name, and cast out demons in your name,
> and do many deeds of power in your name?" Then I will declare
> to them, "I never knew you; go away from me, you evildoers."
> (Matt 7:21–23)

---

2. I discuss the specific strategies of these different Jewish groups in Part Three.

Part Two:

The Bible's Story of a Better Place

4

God Creates a Very Good Place

I THANK GOD WE live in an age when God's people are increasingly aware of the gospel's bold social vision. Christians are more excited than ever to apply the good news in all kinds of places and ways, from what we do with our bodies, to how we entertain ourselves, to how we care for God's good creation. I don't want to get in the way of this progress, but I do want to refine it. It isn't enough for Christians just to do *something*. We are *God's* people, and we need to understand our role as God's people in the world. It's a matter of obedience.

As believers, we have compelling reasons to be actively involved in the world. But as we pull our heads out of the sands of social irrelevance, it is incredibly easy to stick them somewhere else where they don't belong or to stick them where they do belong *in the wrong way*. It matters *how* we involve ourselves, how we act. It doesn't do the world any good if they can't tell the difference between well-intentioned "activism" and the Christian gospel. Discerning that difference is a wonderful—and challenging—task.

Getting Our Story Straight

Misguided as it is, our desire to make the world better flows from good intentions. On the surface, it seems completely biblical. It comes from a certain way of reading Scripture. That way of reading the Bible goes something like this:

1. God created a very good world and called humans to look after its wellbeing.

2. Humans acted so sinfully that creation itself was broken, too. In response, God set apart the descendants of Abraham to do something about that brokenness.

3. Though Abraham's descendants failed to make this world a better place, God sent Jesus to cast a clearer vision of world betterment. After doing so, Jesus died on the cross to conquer sin and death—the very things that were keeping this world from becoming the better place God intended it to be.

4. God did not want Jesus to fix this world by himself, so he gathered Abraham's willing descendants, empowered them by his Spirit, enlarged their ranks to include all ethnic groups, and sent them into all nations to continue his work.

5. Jesus will return someday and complete the task of world betterment.

According to this way of telling of the Bible story, today's church finds itself somewhere in the middle of stage four. By the wisdom and power of Jesus, we have been sent into all nations to announce what he has done, to continue making this world a better place, and to anticipate his return to finish what he started and reward those who have helped him. This is one of the most common ways of telling our story.

The fact that so many preachers and teachers tell the Bible story this way is a vast improvement over how it has been told in the past. You are probably familiar with some of the older tellings that ignore the part God's people play in the story. They focus on how God sent Jesus to die on the cross and save individuals from their sins so they can go to heaven after they die. Such tellings usually have three parts: creation, fall, and redemption. God created a good world, humans corrupted it, and God sent Jesus to fix it. God's people must lead other people to Jesus so he can save them from their sins and grant them everlasting life.

This three-part, simplistic version of the Bible story has led God's people to run away from society, whether by retreating to "safe" spaces and barring the gates against the world or by simply giving the world the silent treatment. Both are ways of stone-walling rather than serving. The more recent five-stage version has led God's people in the opposite direction: to run toward the world, eager to do something about its problems. Both ways of recounting the salvation story contain important elements of truth—especially regarding the nature of the problem and the central-ity of Jesus in solving it. Yet neither adequately captures the role God's people play in salvation history according to Scripture.

Any time you summarize and simplify the Bible, you have to make choices about which details to include. That's inevitable. The problem is that these versions do not give us details about the precise responsibil-ity God has given his people. Getting the Bible story straight is vital for understanding the church's role. Because it's so important, I dedicate the rest of Part Two to telling the story in a way that focuses specifically on God's people and their role, beginning with creation.

The Goodness of Creation

Interestingly enough, Genesis 1 and 2 give us unique angles from which we can view creation. Each chapter briefly describes how things were in this world before it went bad and needed to get better.

Genesis 1 describes creation using the seven-day week. God works for six days and rests on the seventh. This "seven days" angle raises all sorts of interesting questions. We need to pay attention to the details here, especially because the account we're studying is so familiar.

Notice how in Genesis 1 the same phrase appears after God finishes each day's work: "And God saw that it was good" (vv. 4, 10, 12, 18, 21, 25). It is *good* that creation has light and dark, waters and sky, dry land and vegetation. It is *good* that lights fill the sky, birds fly in the air, fish swim the waters, and various animals and humans inhabit the land. Also notice that everything must be put in its proper place. It's only after the sixth day of work that God is satisfied and declares his completed work *very good* (v. 31).

This declaration is an important detail. It tells us that our yearning for a better place doesn't come from a defect in God's creation. It also tells us that the physical universe isn't the product of a conflict that splits the spiritual realm. Our bodies are not cages for our souls that would other-wise be flying free with God. Instead, our bodies and the wider created order are the intentional work of a God who succeeded at making things just the way he wanted them to be. We have to look elsewhere in the story to see where things unravel.

Genesis 1 does introduce us to *what* eventually unravels and *who* eventually pulls at the thread. Humans are responsible. We are named last of all creation in verse 26. God creates humans alone in his image and likeness. Why would God set us apart in this way?

To answer that question, we have to keep reading the rest of the story. Even though creation is "very good," it's not quite complete. There's more to the story here. God has a task for his good creatures: be fruitful, multiply, and fill the earth. Each species is created with the ability to pro-create. Plants and trees multiply using seeds they produce and the sun, soil, and water that God provides. God fashioned humans and animals in gendered pairs that allow them to reproduce, and he gives them various forms of vegetation as their food.

All of these things are raw materials, ingredients. By themselves, in-gredients aren't enough. You have to make something with them. Genesis 1 tells us that creation reaches its full potential only when all creatures properly populate their domains. Birds must fill the air, sea creatures must populate the waters, and humans and animals must settle through-out all habitable land. Only humans, however, are commissioned to get the earth into proper order.

The task of filling the earth comes with potential for conflict. As each species multiplies, spreads, and fills, it inevitably reaches a point where its ability to grow is hampered by the presence of other species. The various species have to negotiate population limits and territorial boundaries if they are to share space peacefully.

Other ancient religions discuss the task of ruling the earth, which God gives to humans in Genesis 1. In some religions, various celestial bodies were in charge of the cosmos. In Egypt, the sun was supreme. Ancient Mesopotamians often believed that a divine figurehead was ulti-mately in charge and that lesser deities fought for control and took turns wielding influence over creaturely affairs.

On the ground, it often played out that a few humans held a mo-nopoly on societal power and wielded absolute authority over creation. These primitive kings or warlords claimed an exclusive relationship to whatever deities were supposedly in charge of their realm. These rulers alone bore the divine image. They were typically male, and they believed that the gods ordained their dynasty or culture to govern their region, if not the entire world.

This is one of the areas where Genesis 1 is unique. It states that *all* humans bear God's image—not just royalty, not just the wealthy elite, and not just males. The reason is evident when we examine the passage within its immediate context:

Then God said, "Let us make humankind in our *image*, according to our *likeness*; and let them have *dominion* over the fish of the sea, and over the birds of the air, and over the cattle, and over all the wild animals of the earth, and over every creeping thing that creeps upon the earth." So God created humankind in his *image*, in the *image* of God he created them; male and female he created them. God blessed them, and God said to them, "Be fruitful and multiply, and fill the earth and *subdue* it; and have *dominion* over the fish of the sea and over the birds of the air and over every living thing that moves upon the earth" (Gen 1:26–28).

Twice these verses affirm that humans were made in God's image, and both times they go on to say that God granted humans dominion over the rest of creation. God created all humans in his image precisely because he wanted the entire race to share responsibility for creation. There is no superior class, ethnic group, gender, or territory. Humans must learn to share authority and responsibility in ways that affirm and uphold the dignity of all humans.

The sun and moon aren't going to step in and mediate conflict. No bird, fish, or four-legged animal will lead the way as God's creatures multiply, fill the earth, and eventually bump into one another. Only humans possess the authority and ability it takes to organize this world the way God intended.

Limits within Creation

The second chapter of Genesis tells a remarkably similar story. One God makes everything without complications or struggle. Everything has its place. Humans are uniquely responsible to look after creation. There is no conflict or deprivation among the creatures. Males and females perfectly suit one another and share responsibility for looking after their land.

Something new also enters into the picture: the concept of limits. Adam is told that he may eat of every tree in the garden, except for one. The forbidden tree is associated with knowledge of good and evil. It also represents limitations on human dominion. Adam cannot do whatever he wants. Dominion is not a blank check. All humans must accept that God alone is ultimately in control. God knows things that we don't, and any authority we wield is on loan from him.

The world of Genesis 1 and 2 didn't need to be made better. It only needed humans to exercise their God-given responsibility to unfold its wonderful potential.

The Dominion Question

Before continuing to tell the story of a better place, we must pause to raise a question. This question is not posed by Genesis itself. It is raised by many who are committed to making this world a better place. As the story unfolds, we see that humanity falls, the image of God is tarnished, Jesus redeems God's image by reflecting it perfectly, and humans are invited to conform to his image.

Does all of this mean that the church's job is to reclaim the lost image and, with it, the responsibility to oversee creation? Does being reborn in Christ reposition believers to rule over creation in ways that are unique to us?

In a pre-fallen world, dominion meant overseeing the development of society and then maintaining it properly. By the time of Jesus, humans had been carrying out this mandate for a very long time. The earth, seas, and skies were mostly filled with their respective creatures, and humans exercised unique authority throughout the process.

Because of sin, however, the world had become a much worse place. Authority was not distributed equally throughout humanity. An elite minority exercised a monopoly over mechanisms of power. Conflict, war, deprivation, and widespread oppression followed.

In this fallen condition, exercising dominion means something different from the original mandate. Global structures for organizing society and maintaining a balanced ecosystem between various species already exist. Dominion in this context therefore means redirecting a snowball that is already rolling downhill at a steady clip. It means leading this world in a better direction in hopes of making it a better place.

This could entail entering existing power structures with new insights from Christ to make them better. It could also mean creating new and better structures to replace the old corrupt ones. Either way, in a developed fallen world, exercising dominion means rolling up our sleeves, getting involved, and making this world a better place.

This train of thought typically comes with a certain way of telling the Bible story between Eden and Jesus. Since humans corrupted everything and the flood didn't really change things, God called Abraham to create a people whose job it was to resume the dominion mandate and make the world a better place. Unfortunately, so the story goes, the Israelites didn't follow God's instructions very well. Things only got worse, which is why God eventually sent Jesus.

According to the popular dominion doctrine, Jesus goes above and beyond this mandate. His task was to make this world better *and* to save it. This salvation account, combined with the creation account, leads to a twofold commission for God's people: the Great Commission and the Cultural Commission. The Great Commission authorizes us to make Christlike disciples of all nations. The Cultural Commission authorizes us to reform fallen cultures and create new ones. It essentially has us making this world a better place.

This entire line of thinking is plausible. Conceptually it makes perfect sense. It is little wonder it has gained a wide following. But it is not the only way to interpret Scripture, and so it needs to be tested. If this way of reading was the backbone of the Bible story, we would expect to find it throughout the narrative. We would see the narrative arc of dominion lost, recovered, lost again, and recovered again appearing at key points throughout Scripture. We would expect to find the notion of a dual vocation or twofold commission at these same key points. We would especially expect to find them in the fall account, the calling of Abraham, the formation of Israel as a nation after the exodus, the teaching and ministry of Jesus, and in the self-understanding of the apostles and other early church leaders.

But we don't.

5

Humans Corrupt God's Very Good Place

THE GARDEN OF EDEN is a very good place. It is rich in natural resources, lush with vegetation, bustling with creatures, and tended by an ideally suited pair of gardeners. For this reason, people often think of it as the perfect place. But Eden's story does not end with Genesis 2. Genesis 3 launches straightway into creaturely rebellion. God's creatures conspire against their creator right in the middle of paradise.

Conspiracy of Irresponsibility

The story is familiar. The serpent tempts the woman to eat the forbidden fruit. The woman bites and invites her husband to do the same. He accepts. Sin officially enters the world and sets into motion a chain of events that disrupts God's creation and calls forth cries for a better place. It is worth slowing down and tending to the details of this account. It shows us the connection between the origin of sin and its dreadful consequences.

This story contains three sets of actors. The serpent represents the animal kingdom. He is introduced as the wisest of the animals (3:1). Eve and Adam represent humanity, which has been appointed to serve and guard creation (2:15). Animals and humans have in common that they are living beings. They are what Hebrew refers to as *nefesh* or living creatures. They possess lifeblood, and God gives them plants as food (1:30). The fruit represents inanimate creation, as does the soil.

The language in Genesis 3, in its original context, would not have conjured up notions of spiritual warfare. While people often focus on the serpent solely as Satan in disguise, the whole framework of Genesis 1–3 leads us to focus on the fact that the serpent is an animal. It is a creature who has *not* been given responsibility over creation. Yet it entices humans—who *are* responsible—to exceed their proper limits.

Whatever else this chapter may be saying to later Christians, it is first and foremost an account of fallen responsibility amid God's good creation. The three sets of actors stand in a different sort of relationship to responsibility. On one side of the spectrum are humans. They have been given authority, but that authority comes with responsibility and therefore limits. On the other side is the fruit. As an inanimate object, the fruit cannot act. It can only be acted upon. It can be an accessory to a crime, but not a criminal.

Between them is the serpent, the most intriguing figure. Like the humans, it is a thinking, choosing, speaking agent. As such, it is not merely an accessory to the crime, but an accomplice. Yet as an animal it has not been given authority, responsibility, or even limits. Without humans to guide or contain them, animals are free to go where they wish and do what they wish. Left to their own devices, animals will steal, kill, and "sleep around" without guilt or thought for how their actions affect the world, other animals, or humans.

The serpent may have already eaten of the fruit without receiving divine censure. God never said that animals could not eat from the forbidden tree. This may explain why the serpent was so wise and how it arrived at the conclusion that eating the fruit does not lead to death. After all, it is still alive. Or, the serpent's motives could have been worse. It could have been seeking to bring humanity down to its own level of irresponsibility. That would, in turn, elevate the serpent's place in the creaturely pecking order.

Regardless of its origins, motives, or experiences, the serpent tempts humans to act like animals that are morally unaccountable for their actions. It tempts them to forsake their proper role as responsible caretakers of all creation—and they bite. The first pair of humans plunges headlong into irresponsibility by declaring independence from God. Only under the creator's direction and authority is dominion properly exercised. Outside of it, as we will see, dominion becomes domination and responsibility becomes tyranny.

Curses and Consequences

The consequences of human irresponsibility were disastrous for the entire created order. God's approach to their disobedience is telling. He confronts Adam first, which indicates that Adam is most responsible for this offense. We are not told this has anything to do with his maleness. We only know that God delivered the prohibition against eating from the tree of knowledge directly to him (2:17). God also holds the woman responsible. After Adam passes the buck her way, God questions her as to what happened. She, in turn, blames the serpent.

Interestingly, God does not engage the serpent in conversation. This must have been a terrible blow to the serpent's ego. It failed to achieve the status of humans after all. God refused to dignify its manipulative attempt at self-promotion by addressing it in a humanlike way.

Nonetheless, all parties suffer the consequences: the responsible humans, the non-responsible accomplice, and the inanimate accessory. The consequences are of two sorts. One is a natural outcome of the choice to sin. It is not something that God initiates, but that humans trigger by choosing sin. The other is a divine action that brings about a specific change in creaturely existence. This action is often as much gracious initiative as it is punishment.

It is helpful to distinguish between these natural outcomes and gracious initiatives. God's pronouncement in Genesis 3 is not the beginning of a string of wrath-filled actions that an angry God unleashes upon his wayward creatures. It is not as if God first curses the original sinners, next floods the earth, then annihilates the Canaanites, and eventually anyone else who rubs him the wrong way. One doesn't have to be a Jew or a Christian to see that this sort of interpretation gets the story all wrong.

Remember that after God expels Adam and Eve from Eden, he sews clothing for them and helps Eve bear their first child (4:1). Remember that after Cain kills his brother Abel, God protects Cain from those who would kill him in an effort to make the world a safer place (4:15). Remember that God was grieved by the sin that required him to flood the earth, not angered by humans and ready to unleash his pent up fury (6:6).

God's poetic declaration in Genesis 3 contains both a description of the mess humans made of God's world and a description of how God begins to clean up that mess by making countermoves that preserve his original purposes for creation. The contributions humans make are stated as matters of fact. God's countermoves are sometimes stated in the language of curses.

The Serpent

God's first countermove is to curse the serpent by demoting it to its belly (v. 14). It is now the lowest of all creatures. This demotion in status may indicate that God perceived the serpent's motive to be an elevation in status. This is bad for the serpent's agenda, but good for humans. An enlarged gap between humans and animals ensures that these two parties will no longer conspire together against God's authority. Should humans sin again, it won't be because the serpent made them do it.

The relational proximity that allowed an animal to lead humans to sin is replaced with enmity. Animals—especially snakes—will strike at human heels and inflict injury, but humans will ultimately triumph over them (v. 15). It's not as if God instigates every skirmish between humans and animals. God does not throw humans and creatures in a cage together, sound a bell, and then watch them tear each other apart. Rather, because of sin, the harmony that once existed between all God's creatures was seriously disrupted, and it has been this way ever since. God enlarged the gap between humans and animals for our own good, and we lash out against one another without divine provocation.

The Woman

God then acts by increasing the pain women experience in childbirth (v. 16). Curse language is not used here as with the serpent. God had something else in mind. The dispute that led to human independence from God had to do with life and death. God warned that eating from the forbidden tree would lead to death. By placing the tree of life in the garden, God gave humans and perhaps other creatures the opportunity to enjoy life without end. Eve weighed the benefit of eating the forbidden fruit against the risk. She then chose knowledge and the possibility of death.

Like the serpent's status violation, this poor choice required a divine corrective. God institutes a painful gestation period for humans, followed by high risk labor and delivery. Though this could be interpreted as mere punishment, it also instilled in humans a deeper appreciation for the gift of life. Human existence is not like an annual cycle of crops that may be reaped in large quantities on a cyclical basis. Life is precious and fragile, not to be taken for granted. It is worth the cost of respecting the limits that God places on our dominion. Morning sickness, miscarriages, dying mothers, and various forms of infant mortality have been with us ever since.

The next consequence of sin is not presented as a divine initiative. God tells Eve that her *desire* will be for her husband and that he will *rule over* her (v. 16). God doesn't say, "I will make you desire your husband and command him to rule over you." The sentence is not constructed that way in the original language. Importantly, the words for "desire" and "rule" have many connotations, some positive, some negative. But these same words are used in the next chapter of Genesis. There they describe sin's *desire* to overtake Cain and Cain's need to *rule over* it (4:7). It is most likely, then, that God is warning Eve that her choice to sin has created a world of conflict between men and women. Unfortunately for her gender, men will typically dominate that relationship. Most women can only long for that sort of power. Eve inadvertently traded the equal dominion of Genesis 1–2 for a battle of the sexes that women often lose.

God did not instigate this. Rather, sin created a world in which shared leadership is rare and those with more power rule over those with less. This means not only the fall of women from power, but the fall of power into domination. The rich will dominate the poor, the strong will dominate the weak, and humans will dominate animals and exploit creation. In most cases, the weaker party longs for the power of the stronger. God does not sanction this state of affairs. He simply warns that it is the new terrain that all creatures will have to navigate.

The Man

When God addresses Adam, he refrains from cursing him directly. Instead, he curses the ground. The decision to eat the forbidden fruit transgressed the limits of human dominion and depreciated the value of human life. It also disdained the abundant provisions that God supplied for humans. Adam and Eve lacked nothing in Eden. They had endless rations, but they did not consider them enough. They wanted it all. They spurned the gift of food, just like the gift of life.

So God initiates another corrective: the soil that sustained the tree that produced the fruit that served as an accessory to sin is cursed. It no longer yields fruit in abundance. Humans have to toil arduously to harvest a decent crop. The superior strength that gives men an upper hand in power struggles with women also equips them best to break through the newly hardened soil. Of course, women and animals bear this burden as well. No aspect of creation is immune from the mess that sin has made of this world.

The ultimate consequence of sin is death. The dust out of which God created Adam becomes the tomb of human death and decay. God banishes humans from the garden, which was their only access to the tree of life. Death is now an ongoing reality.

This, too, was a divine initiative, and so a measure of grace. To live forever in a state of sin is a dreadful form of torture (the movie *Groundhog Day* comes to mind). Eternal enmity with the animal kingdom, eternal scratching at hardened soil, eternal domination of the strong over the weak—none of this is what God had in mind for this world. *By ending life in a sin-spoiled world, God creates the necessity and therefore the possibility of a new beginning. He creates the desire for a better place.*

Violence and Promise

After the fall, things rapidly decline. In Genesis 4–6, all the negative consequences of sin unfold. Brother kills brother and defiles the soil with human blood. God has to protect Cain from wider society, which wants to kill him. Alienation from the soil and wider society leads Cain to found a city. This city becomes a place where men take many wives for themselves, continue to kill one another, and multiply vengeance (4:23–24). As humans increase upon the earth, the powerful prey upon the weak by taking wives of whomever they wish. This leads to the rise of a warrior class upon the earth, the Nephilim. These massive mercenaries likely served the whims of primitive kings or warlords who sought to expand their tyrannical reign upon the earth (6:1–4).

The end result is stated concisely in Genesis 6:5: "The LORD saw that the wickedness of humankind was great in the earth, and that every inclination of the thoughts of their hearts was only evil continually." This profoundly impacted creation itself: "the earth was corrupt in God's sight, and the earth was filled with violence . . . for all flesh had corrupted its ways upon the earth" (6:11, 12). The earth had become such a terrible place that "the LORD was sorry that he had made humankind on the earth, and it grieved him to his heart" (6:6).

What did human sin accomplish? It distorted all relationships between humans and God, humans and humans, humans and creation. It placed all of God's creatures on a path to degeneration, decay, and ultimately death. It created a world in which corruption, promiscuity, and violence were so rampant that God destroys nearly all life with a flood in order to begin anew. In flooding the earth, God takes a big step forward in making this world a better place. At the least, he makes it a less bad place.

Still, the root of the problem has not changed, "for the inclination of the human heart is evil from youth" (8:21). What has changed is God's resolve. Immediately after acknowledging that humans remain the same, God vows never again to curse the ground and destroy all creatures on account of human sin. He then promises that the seasonal rhythms of creation will never cease (8:22) and makes a covenant with all creation (9:8–17). The rainbow in the clouds serves as a perpetual reminder of this covenant. It is no coincidence that the Hebrew word for rainbow is the same word as an archer's bow, the ancient weapon of choice. God was symbolically retiring his weapon of mass destruction.[1] In doing so, *he places the burden on himself to find some other way to make a better place of this earth.*

Dominion Revisited

It is worth returning at this point to the notion of dominion so common among Christian activists for a better world. It is often implied that because of sin, the image of God was corrupted and the human race

1. We should not presume that God is only committing in Genesis 9 not to destroy the earth *by water*, as if he was reserving the right to destroy it some other way. In ancient Mesopotamian cosmology, water was *the* way to destroy the earth. They did not believe, as Stoics later on, that this earth was generated by fire and would return to fire. For Mesopotamians, as reflected in Genesis 1, the earth was founded upon the waters and could only return to waters. Fire could only bring local destruction since it would ultimately run out of fuel as it encounters desert or runs into water and is extinguished. This is not contradicted by the reference to burning with fire in 2 Peter 3:10. In that passage the earth is disclosed or revealed, whereas only heavenly elements are burned. Together they convey a refining of God's good creation. The impurities are burned off so the true essence will shine forth all the more brilliantly.

somehow surrendered dominion. This in turn created the need for God to set apart a specific people and entrust world governance to them.

Yet the fall account says nothing of God's image being lost or even distorted. On the contrary, the immediate context of Genesis implies that God's image was successfully transmitted in a fallen world. The genealogy in chapter 5 states that Seth, who was born after the fall, bore the "likeness" and "image" of Adam (v. 3). These two terms deliberately echo 1:26, which talks about humans being made in God's image and likeness. There is no hint here that the image passed along has in any way been compromised. People of Seth's lineage, just like Cain's offspring, will corrupt the earth and incur divine judgment in the flood, but the text makes no connection between human failing and the divine image.

God's image does not resurface again until Genesis 9:6. This passage, which immediately follows the flood, prohibits shedding human blood because "in his own image God made humankind." The flood washes away neither the image of God nor the tendency of humans to sin. The two are simply never connected.

Nowhere in the remainder of Scripture does humanity lose God's image. After Genesis 9, most of the image language in the Old Testament has to do with idolatry. Humans are commanded not to make images of God (Exod 20:4). Most scholars agree that this is partly because humans remain God's sole image bearers. To make a divine image out of inanimate objects cheapens our status as divine image bearers and brings God down to a level far beneath him.

Nor does the New Testament teach that sin has somehow expunged God's image from humans. Colossians 1:15 and 2 Corinthians 4:4 refer to Jesus as God's image, but not to the exclusion of other humans. Colossians 3 exhorts believers to put on the new self that is being renewed in the image of the creator. Our rebirth in Christ gives us the opportunity to image God all over again. But the context here has nothing to do with dominion, power, or rule over creation. The text says nothing about renewed image bearers assuming some sort of responsibility for creation that the rest of humanity gave up through their sinfulness.

In Colossians 3, bearing Christ's image means setting our minds on things that are above (vv. 1–4); dying to sinful behavior (vv. 5–9); clothing ourselves with a new self that is renewed according to the image of the creator (v. 10); renouncing all distinctions rooted in ethnicity, religious heritage, territorial citizenship, and economic status (v. 11); and embracing a life of humility, love, and harmony within the body of Christ (vv.

12–15). Imaging God in this passage has to do with incorporation into a new community where unity in Christ reigns supreme. It has nothing to do with dominion over the old order of things that we have left behind.

Neither does the fall account teach that dominion has been abandoned by or removed from humanity as a species. It simply indicates that dominion has warped into a form of domination in which there are winners and losers. Authority is not evenly distributed in a fallen world the way God intended.

Throughout the Old Testament and into the New Testament, humans continue to serve as the species among all of God's creatures that run things here on earth—even if they mostly run it into the ground. It remains to be seen—when God creates, equips, and commissions his set-apart people—whether he gives them unique power and authority over the earth and commissions them to run things on his behalf.

Spoiler alert: he doesn't.

6

God Uses the Powers to Make This World a Better Place

AT THIS POINT, IT is common for those telling the Bible story to observe simply that things didn't get much better after the flood. God laments that the human heart remains wicked (8:21). Noah gets excessively drunk and his son, Ham, disgraces him when he is vulnerable (9:20–27). And instead of scattering throughout the world like God commanded, a good number of people huddle in one place and strive to make a name for themselves by building the great city of Babel (11:1–9).

Humanity had hoped to build a better place, so the story goes, but God knew better. A city built on human pride would only lead to human oppression. So God spoils their cultural and architectural achievement by confusing their languages and scattering them throughout the world. God alone knows what it takes to make a better place. In Genesis 12, he calls Abraham away from the region where Babel was built and begins to form a chosen people. They are the ones, so it seems, who will make this world a better place.

This way of telling the story is mostly right. Things do fall apart quickly after the flood, and human wickedness, excess, and hubris are clearly to blame. What is wrong with this telling is *what it leaves out* and *what it assumes*. It wrongly assumes that God calls Abraham and his descendants to make this world a better place. We address this faulty assumption in the next chapter. This chapter focuses on what it leaves out, namely, the powers.

Meet the Powers

When recounting any story, it is easy to focus on foreground characters whose heroic actions propel the plot forward. But we shouldn't overlook background characters. Without them, the story makes little sense. When it comes to the Bible story, God not only blesses all nations through Abraham's descendants (foreground); he also uses the powers (background) to make this world a better place. These tasks differ considerably.

"Powers" language comes from the New Testament, especially writings associated with the Apostle Paul. It is a shorthand way of saying "principalities and powers." In some strands of Christian fiction, these entities are equated with demons and devils. They are key characters in tales about spiritual warfare. There is some biblical basis for this, but the biblical emphasis is different from what one finds, for instance, in C. S. Lewis's *Screwtape Letters* and Frank Peretti's *This Present Darkness*.

In a few places, the powers and principalities are heavenly beings with whom humans must contend (Eph 3:10; 6:12). In other places, they are human leaders, religious and political. When such is the case, translators often use the phrase "rulers and authorities" (Rom 13:1–4). This can be misleading. In the original language, the terms translated "principalities and powers" and "rulers and authorities" are identical (*archon* and *exousia*), and with good reason.

In the first-century Jewish and Christian mind-set, heavenly and earthly rulers are connected. God reigns over all creation through a chain of rulers stretching from heaven to earth. God is in charge of archangels who are in charge of lower angels who are in charge of kings who are in charge of governors who are in charge of local rulers who are in charge of cities that are made of families, which are led by parents.

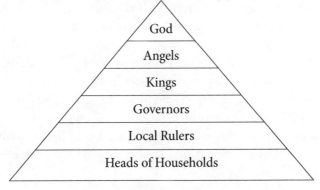

We see the upper end of this chain in Daniel's portrait of heavenly princes that correspond to specific earthly kingdoms (Dan 10:10–21). Persia, Greece, and Israel possess different heavenly representatives. Angels are also linked to human kings in Isaiah 24:21–23 and Psalm 82. In these passages, earthly *and* heavenly rulers come under God's judgment for failing to rule properly over human affairs. The book of Job likely refers to this judgment when it alludes to erring angels (Job 4:18; 15:15). Ancient Jewish texts, like 1 Enoch, continue this line of thinking.

This chain of command deeply impacts human flourishing. Since these authorities came into power in a fallen world, their impact is often negative. That is why humans struggle against them (Eph 6:12). Some of them even strive to separate us from God's love (Rom 8:38–39). So Christ made a spectacle of the powers and triumphed over them on the cross (Col 2:15). Since that time, they are being subjected under Christ's feet, and those that resist will eventually be destroyed (1 Cor 15:24–26).

Appreciate the Powers

We should not think of the powers in purely negative terms. The Apostle Paul writes that they have been created by God through Christ in order to serve God's purposes:

> He [Christ] is the image of the invisible God, the firstborn of all creation; for in him all things in heaven and on earth were created, things visible and invisible, whether thrones or dominions or rulers or powers—all things have been created through him *and for him*. He himself is before all things, and in him all things hold together. (Col 1:15–17)

This is why numerous passages implore Christians to accept the authority of various rulers that are above them—whether kings, governors, masters, parents, or spouses. We are asked to pray for them precisely because what they do impacts the conditions in which we carry out our mission. They have the ability and responsibility to make this world a better place. They do so on God's behalf and for our own good. A sampling of Scripture supports this point:

> Let every person be subject to the governing authorities; for there is no authority except from God, and those authorities that exist have been instituted by God. Therefore whoever resists authority resists what God has appointed, and those who

resist will incur judgment. For rulers are not a terror to good conduct, but to bad. Do you wish to have no fear of the authority? Then do what is good, and you will receive its approval; for it is God's servant for your good. (Rom 13:1–4a)

I urge that supplications, prayers, intercessions, and thanksgivings be made for everyone, for kings and all who are in high positions, so that we may lead a quiet and peaceable life in all godliness and dignity. This is right and is acceptable in the sight of God our Savior, who desires everyone to be saved and to come to the knowledge of the truth. (1 Tim 2:1–4)

For the Lord's sake accept the authority of every human institution, whether of the emperor as supreme, or of governors, as sent by him to punish those who do wrong and to praise those who do right. (1 Pet 2:13–14)

These verses teach us that governing authorities have been instituted by God. They serve God and they serve our good, even though they don't always do what is good for us. When functioning properly they enable us to lead quiet and peaceful lives, help create conditions in which people may be saved, punish wrongdoers, curtail bad conduct, and encourage good conduct. When they carry out their proper function, those under them are free to flourish, including the church. Even Jesus recognizes their power on loan from God (John 19:11).

Peter and the Powers

This basic framework spans the entirety of Scripture, from Genesis to Revelation. Here I zoom in on one book that makes it particularly clear. First Peter acknowledges that angelic rulers and governing authorities are not the only powers we must respect: "For the Lord's sake accept the authority of *every human institution*" (2:13). Peter then goes on to encourage all believers to submit to public officials, slaves to submit to unbelieving masters, and wives to accept the authority of their unbelieving husbands.

We encounter the powers in the workforce and in the household. All bosses are powers. All parents are powers. All educators are powers. They are "human institutions" that strive to bring order to society. They seek to make the world a better place. Sometimes they even succeed. That is why many of them are viewed as benefactors even though they abuse their authority by lording over the people they've been called to serve (Luke 22:25).

Peter was not superimposing an oppressive Roman hierarchy on the church's life together. He was reminding believers that God uses fallen powers outside of Christ to keep order in a chaotic world. He was instructing those who had been set free by Christ (1 Pet 2:16) not to impede the powers' work but to be witnesses to all unbelievers, including the powers (2:12, 15). The Apostle Paul also implored the church to be a positive witness to the powers, even the heavenly ones (Eph 3:10).

Peter is not naïve about the powers' fallenness, nor does he see them as the future of world history. He recognizes that all "angels, authorities, and powers" are being subjugated under Christ (1 Pet 3:22). He affirms that our inheritance is not with the powers, but is being kept in heaven for us and will be brought to us when Christ is revealed (1:3–13). Peter was neither an imperial sycophant nor an anti-imperial rebel. He was a devout Christian who realized that the church and state are different institutions, each with an important role to play. He implored God's people to stick to their proper calling and to allow the powers to stick to theirs.

Genesis and the Powers

You may be wondering what this has to do with Genesis. How did we get from Babel to apostle? Simply put, God's providential work to make this world a better place through the powers has deep Old Testament roots. It goes back as far as Noah's day. Long before he called Abraham, God responds to human wickedness in four ways.

(1) God shortens human life-spans. If the genealogy of Genesis 5 is any indication, the earliest humans lived very long lives, up to nearly a thousand years. The problem is that they lived long lives in the context of warlords who were carving up the earth, tyrannizing commoners, and extending their reigns with the help of giant warriors (6:1–2). Life under an oppressive ruler is bad enough. Now imagine Hitler living over 500 years! By capping human life-spans at around 120 years (6:3), God breaks the longevity and stability of oppressive ruling dynasties. A fallen world cannot have order without rulers, but there is no need for them to rule more than forty or so years, the ideal length for the reign of a judge or king.[1]

(2) God disrupts the negative momentum of wickedness. Creation had been barreling out of control since Adam. It was on a collision course with itself. The best way forward, from God's point of view, was to purge

1. See Judg 8:28; 1 Sam 4:18; 1 Kgs 2:11; 11:42; 2 Kgs 12:1.

the earth and start all over again with a small sampling of each species, which God preserved on the ark. This, too, may be considered a gracious divine initiative. Consider the example of a terminally ill pregnant woman whose body is rapidly deteriorating. The most loving thing for the doctor to do—and the very thing the mother would want—is to take the life of the dying mother so the child may live. In the same way, taking the life of all creatures that were wrapped up in destroying this world may have been the only way for God to allow all creatures to repopulate and refill the earth. Though the flood does not erase evil from the human heart, it dramatically slows humanity's self-destruction, which creates time for God's other initiatives to take effect.

(3) God underscores the sacredness of life. He does this first by placing the dread of humans upon all animals (9:2).[2] Apparently humans were killing and consuming animals—blood and all—before the flood. Though God permits humans to eat animals from this point forward, we may not drink their blood (vv. 3–4). All lifeblood is sacred, even animals'. This passage anticipates Israel's sacrificial system. Not just anyone could shed animal blood. Early on, only priests could slaughter animals, both for ritual offerings and common meals. Every act of bloodshed is a sacred, ritual act (Lev 17).

If animal life is sacred to God, how much more humans! So God places limits on blood vengeance (Gen 9:5–6). To appreciate why, we need to look at the backstory. When people want to kill the first killer, God protects him with the threat of revenge. Anyone who kills Cain would be avenged sevenfold (4:15). God reserves for himself the right to take life. Shortly after, Lamech kills a man. Rather than show remorse, he plays God and takes vengeance into his own hands, saying, "If Cain is avenged sevenfold, truly Lamech seventy-sevenfold" (4:24).

This trend must have escalated beyond control. By the time of the flood, God observes that the whole earth is filled with violence. In fact, it is because of such violence that he destroys the earth (6:13). This is the proper context for interpreting God's postdiluvian (post-flood) declaration:

2. The text does not say explicitly that *God* placed the dread of humans on animals, but it is a reasonable conclusion. The text introduces animal dread of humans as a new thing. Yet the fact that God forbids the consumption of animal blood immediately after the flood suggests that humans were consuming it before the flood. If human aggression alone were the initial cause of animal dread, it would thus have been present before the flood and not a new thing here. This leaves God as the most likely agent.

> For your own life blood I will surely require a reckoning: from
> every animal I will require it and from human beings, each one
> for the blood of another, I will require a reckoning for human
> life. Whoever sheds the blood of a human, by a human shall
> that person's blood be shed; for in his own image God made
> humankind. (Gen 9:5–6)

The point of this passage is not that humans are now free to kill people. As we just saw, humans had been exercising that liberty for a long time. The point is that *only* a killer is to be killed. No one else! Not the killer *and* his family. Not the killer *and* his closest friends. The punishment may not exceed the crime. Humans may not multiply vengeance like Lamech and his violent successors. God reins in human violence by declaring all blood sacred.

(4) Finally, God scatters humans throughout the world with diverse cultures. After the flood, God recommissions the human race to multiply and fill the earth. The genealogy of Genesis 10 shows that Noah's descendants eventually scatter throughout the earth. It shows the founding of prominent nations near and far, including Egypt, Assyria, Babylon, and Persia. These were the mighty powers of the ancient world.

Not all humans obey God's command to scatter. Though Genesis 10 simply states that Nimrod founded Babel and several other major cities, the next chapter gives an in-depth account of Babel's origins. Its founders have no intention of scattering and planting multiple cities. They want to stay in one place and build a massive urban power center. If the kings' recently shortened life-spans can't ensure a lasting kingdom, perhaps a mighty fortified city could.

God knew this would only lead to more domination and oppression. So he confuses the builders' languages and forces them to scatter. Multiplying languages means multiplying cultures. As humans migrate, they develop their own language, customs, politics, and economics. They forge a unique way of life that they grow to love and desire to maintain.

The more powerful cultures, of course, want to force their way of life on others and expand the scope of their influence. The multiplicity of languages limits this. Each culture will do whatever it takes to keep powerful nations from expanding into their territory.

It is no coincidence that Babel's founder, Nimrod, is described as a "mighty man" (10:9) whose people seek to make a "name" for themselves (11:4). Before the flood, the earth was populated with "mighty men" of "name" (6:4) who filled the earth with violence. In scattering the builders of Babel and creating a plurality of cultures, God takes decisive steps toward keeping the world from reverting back to the horrible place it became before the flood. *To make the world a better place, God institutes a plurality of competing powers—an international system of checks and balances.*

Powers in the Old Testament

Throughout the Old Testament, God uses this diverse array of nations for a variety of purposes. He uses Egypt to help the Israelites and others survive an extended famine in Palestine. Though God's people end up suffering terribly under Egyptian enslavement, God uses their time in Egypt to multiply them numerically while preserving their unique identity.

After they take possession of the promised land, the Israelites break their covenant with God. So God uses neighboring peoples, such as the Philistines, to punish them and lead them back to him. Several centuries later, the Israelites have kings who lead them further astray. God then uses Assyria to punish the northern kingdom and Babylon to punish the southern kingdom. These nations didn't see themselves as God's instruments, but God did. Hear God's words through the prophet Isaiah:

> Ah, Assyria, the rod of my anger—the club in their hands is my fury! Against a godless nation I send him, and against the people of my wrath I command him, to take spoil and seize plunder, and to tread them down like the mire of the streets. But this is not what he intends, nor does he have this in mind; but it is in his heart to destroy, and to cut off nations not a few (Isa 10:5–7).

It is equally important to observe that God also uses pagan nations to keep one another in check. He uses Babylon, for instance, to topple Assyria, and Persia to defeat Babylon. This is God's doing. God's people had to learn to accept this, which was not easy. The prophet Habakkuk was repulsed by the fact that God chose Babylon to punish Israel (Hab 1). He agreed that Israel deserved punishing, but he couldn't stomach God using anyone besides his "righteous" people to accomplish his purposes. God set him straight (ch. 2).

The Main Point

What does all this have to do with the church's misguided desire to make the world a better place?

My point is this: *The tasks of keeping sin in check, meeting basic needs, and making the world a better place are crucial for human thriving, but they are tasks that God has assigned to ordinary human power structures.* Most people assume that the powers hold world history in their hands. The powers are the movers and shakers. What they do has potential to make life better for all people. This is why everyone gets so excited around election seasons and regime changes. What rulers do appears to be most important.

God's people have always been tempted to be like these powers. We often assume that because they are fallen and often leave their work undone, it must be our job to pick up the slack. Who better to fix this world than those who are intimately familiar with God's will?

Israel was tempted to think this way. When Babylon needed to be punished, Israelite captives needed to be set free, and Jerusalem needed to be restored—God's people mourned that they could not pull this off. So the prophet Isaiah reminded them of their proper place, saying, "*It is too light a thing* that you should be my servant to raise up the tribes of Jacob and to restore the survivors of Israel; I will give you as a light to the nations, that my salvation may reach to the end of the earth" (49:6).

It's not that it wasn't important for Israel to be restored. It's simply that this is not a task that Israel was called to accomplish. God had in mind to use someone else. He uses Persian kings to defeat Babylon, send the exiles home, and even sponsor the rebuilding of Jerusalem's temple and walls.

That is precisely the point. God can always find wealthy benefactors and worldly rulers to meet needs and organize the masses. There will always be prosperous pagans, high-profile humanitarians, middle-class do-gooders, and upwardly mobile politicians who want to secure a lasting name by making this world a slightly better place. It appears to be God's will to use such people to do this very thing, whatever their intentions may be.

What God wants from his set-apart people, however, is much more important according to Scripture. Only we can do it. According to Isaiah, that important task involves being a light to the nations that will reach the ends of the earth. "It is too light a thing" for us to focus on anything else.

This brings us back to Abraham.

7

God Forms a People to Prepare for a Better Place

Up until this point in the Bible story, God's people don't really exist as a set-apart group. Genesis 1–11 speaks about the human race more generally. We encounter righteous individuals like Enoch and Noah who pleased God, but they are not introduced as members of a set apart community. They are outstanding individuals among their families and the human race.

God showed deep concern for all creation. When humans nearly destroyed it, he took drastic measures to save it from immediate catastrophe and future threats posed by violent humans. Shorter life-spans, life-honoring laws, cultural diversity, and an international system of checks and balances serve to preserve creation from ultimate collapse. The powers play the lead human role in this work of preservation.

As important as preservation is for human thriving, it is not God's only work. His other work is more important. Though the powers maintain the conditions that make this other work possible, it is not their responsibility. Sole responsibility belongs to the set apart people that God begins to form in Genesis 12.

The Founding Charters of God's People

God's people were named after the patriarch Jacob, whom God named Israel. Their most widely recognized founders, however, are Abraham and Moses. Though the lives of all three men were remarkable and instrumental, the founding charters of Abraham and Moses truly set them apart.

To Abraham God said, "Go from your country and your kindred and your father's house to the land that I will show you. I will make of you a great nation, and I will bless you, and make your name great, so that you will be a blessing. I will bless those who bless you, and the one who curses you I will curse; and in you all the families of the earth shall be blessed" (Gen 12:1–3).

To Moses he said, "Thus you shall say to the house of Jacob, and tell the Israelites: You have seen what I did to the Egyptians, and how I bore you on eagles' wings and brought you to myself. Now therefore, if you obey my voice and keep my covenant, you shall be my treasured possession out of all the peoples. Indeed, the whole earth is mine, but you shall be for me a priestly kingdom and a holy nation" (Exod 19:3–6).

These are the first two statements that God makes about his people's nature and mission. He begins both by commanding his people to move away from thriving empires that represented the height of civilization in their day. Abraham must leave Babylon, and the Israelites must flee Egypt. In both cases, God leads them to Palestine where they will forge a different sort of identity. They cannot be a mere extension of the empires they are leaving behind.

The second thing God says in these statements is that his people are especially blessed by him. God promises to make Abraham's name great and to make him a great nation. God will bless him so much that his offspring will be a visible demonstration of divine blessing. Others will look to them and see what it means to be blessed. God describes Moses' people as especially treasured. Though the whole world belongs to God, he considers the Israelites his prized possession. What an honor!

The final thing God says in both charters is that his people will relate to other nations in a unique way. Somehow all the earth's inhabitants will be blessed through Abraham, though he was never told exactly how. Somehow the slaves that Moses freed from Egypt will be a priestly kingdom and a holy nation. These two titles may be different ways of saying the same thing. Holy means set apart according to God's standards for God's purposes. Priests were set apart to serve God. Though they are set apart *from* other people, they are also set apart *for* those same people.

Statements like these may be interpreted as divine mandates to make this world a better place. How better to bless and serve all nations than to find and fix whatever ails them. Yet Israel's charters are quite vague about *how* God's people will bless this world. If we assume, on the one hand, that this world needs a people to mend and manage it, we need only read between the lines that this is their priestly function. On the other hand, if we assume that all nations need to know that God will destroy this world and that their only hope to survive is to relocate to heaven, then preparing all nations for imminent departure could be their means of blessing. Neither interpretation will do.

These charters are generic enough that we can read just about any agenda into them. To guard against this, we need to keep reading the story while also working to identify the story's own agenda. How does God equip his people for their unique service? What does he commission them to do? How does he commission them to do it? What sort of things does God rebuke them for doing? What does he fault them for leaving undone? These sorts of questions bring us closer to the heart of God's intentions for his people.

The Better Way of Torah

Any biblical attempt to find answers must begin with Torah. If God's founding statements to Abraham and Moses were Israel's charter, Torah was their constitution. Torah is not simply a body of laws that regulates behavior. It is the way of life to which God called his people.

Though God's laws are scattered throughout Exodus, Leviticus, and Numbers, they are packaged together conveniently in the book of Deuteronomy. They are sandwiched between two statements that help future Israelites understand their nature and purpose. These statements reveal much about how God's people understood their place in this world.

The first statement appears near the beginning of Moses' sermon:

> See, just as the LORD my God has charged me, I now teach you statutes and ordinances for you to observe in the land that you are about to enter and occupy. You must observe them diligently, for this will show your wisdom and discernment to the peoples, who, when they hear all these statutes, will say, "Surely this great nation is a wise and discerning people!" For what other great nation has a god so near to it as the LORD our God is whenever we call to him? And what other great nation has statutes and ordinances as just as this entire law that I am setting before you today? (Deut 4:5–8)

The second statement appears near the end:

> See, I have set before you today life and prosperity, death and adversity. If you obey the commandments of the LORD your God that I am commanding you today, by loving the LORD your God, walking in his ways, and observing his commandments, decrees, and ordinances, then you shall live and become numerous, and the LORD your God will bless you in the land that you are entering to possess. But if your heart turns away and you do not hear, but are led astray to bow down to other gods and serve them, I declare to you today that you shall perish; you shall not live long in the land that you are crossing the Jordan to enter and possess. I call heaven and earth to witness against you today that I have set before you life and death, blessings and curses. Choose life so that you and your descendants may live, loving the LORD your God, obeying him, and holding fast to him; for that means life to you and length of days, so that you may live in the land that the LORD swore to give to your ancestors, to Abraham, to Isaac, and to Jacob. (Deut 30:15–20)

These passages reveal how God intended to bless his chosen people. His blessing was not arbitrary favor. It was the way of life into which God welcomed the Israelites. Had they followed his instructions, they would have thrived in the land he gave them. Deuteronomy 28 indicates that they would be blessed in every way—in city and field, children and cattle, barns and baskets. No nation would dominate them, nor would they depend on other nations for their sustenance. God would richly supply all their needs.

How, then, would other nations be blessed though God's people? These verses are not exactly clear. They do say that the nations would notice. They would see the superior way of life that God's people lived, and they would be impressed. God's people would be renowned for their wisdom and discernment. To use the words of Isaiah, they would be a light to all nations (49:6). But the nations wouldn't be content to look from a distance:

> In days to come the mountain of the LORD's house shall be established as the highest of the mountains, and shall be raised above the hills; all the nations shall stream to it. Many peoples shall come and say, "Come, let us go up to the mountain of the LORD, to the house of the God of Jacob; that he may teach us his ways and that we may walk in his paths." For out of Zion shall

go forth instruction, and the word of the LORD from Jerusalem
(Isa 2:2–3).

Notice how God's people come to bless and instruct the nations according to these verses. The order is crucial:

1. God takes his people away from the nations and makes them his own nation.

2. God's people order their lives according to God's instructions.

3. God's people thrive due to the superior way of life that he gives them and the blessings he pours upon them.

4. The nations notice and are impressed, having never before seen such a life.

5. The nations decide on their own to come to where God is blessing his people in order to learn this way of life from him.

It's important to note what God's people do *not* do. They do not come up with their own plan for making the world better. They do not engineer their own path to success. They do not devise a marketing strategy and promote it among the nations. Nor do they presume because of their prosperity and unique relationship to God that they are entitled to rule over other nations. They do not seek to enlarge their territory by absorbing inferior nations. They do not colonize other nations for their own good or head up an international coalition. *They simply live how God calls them to live. They don't try to make the world a better place. They humbly accept that God is making them into a better place.*

The Path Not Chosen

That is the plan that God set forth for his people. He didn't equip them to do anything else. He certainly didn't place them in the Fertile Crescent's prime real estate. That land was already occupied by Egypt, Assyria, and Babylon. Israel's land only flows with milk and honey when God showers it with his blessings (Deut 11:10–12). Otherwise, it's back to Egypt when the next major famine strikes.

God didn't equip the Israelites with a comprehensive plan for national security, territorial expansion, or international diplomacy. He told them to avoid other nations, stick to their own territory, and rely upon him as their national defense. God would either assemble an ad hoc untrained militia to fight their battles (Num 10:9) or he would unleash supernatural forces upon invading armies (Josh 6:5; 10:11; 23:10; 24:12). Though other nations believed that their gods fought for them, none of them trusted their gods enough to forego forming their own highly trained standing army. Only Israel would do that—at least in the beginning—and it would take tremendous faith!

Nor did God give his people a stable form of civil government. Torah divided the land into twelve equal territories, each of which had its own elders, judges, prophets, and priests. There was no capital city or centrally located temple, though they maintained a sacred mobile tent. Should they decide to crown a king, he could not make marital alliances with neighboring nations. Nor could he fortify his reign with the latest military technology or accumulate great wealth in order to impress his subjects and intimidate potential invaders. The only king God would allow, according to Deuteronomy 17, is a symbolic figurehead who must remain subject to Torah and defer to the priests' interpretation of it.

In short, God did not build his people into a nation that could aspire to the superpower status of neighboring empires. At best, they would be a relatively small and quirky nation that appears to the nations to have something of an unhealthy codependency upon their deity.

Unfortunately, the Israelites came to see it that way as well. The book of Judges tells the story of how they quickly abandoned their constitution, incurred divine cursing, and floundered as a result. Rather than repent of their ways or forsake God altogether, they crafted a hybrid approach to nationhood. Beginning in 1 Samuel 8, they combined select aspects of Torah with kingship like the nations.

This brought some measure of stability and prosperity, especially when compared to smaller nations nearby. By the time of Solomon, Israel had acquired its own king, its own standing army, a standard approach to diplomacy, and a socioeconomic system with a wealthy class that could impress neighboring nations.

God was not impressed. As he predicted through Moses (Deut 31–32), the whole project began to crumble under the weight of its own inadequacies. The commoners revolted against oppressive nobles, and the kingdom split in two. Though each kingdom lasted for a time, a few centuries later, larger nations came along and conquered them one after the other.

Prophetic Insight

Of course, God did not surrender his people without a fight. He sent prophets to call them back to Torah and warn them of the perilous consequences of their waywardness. These prophets provide a valuable window into God's heart for Israel. What God found lacking in his people speaks volumes about what he originally intended for them.

The prophets' unified testimony is that God's people failed to live out Torah. They failed to rely upon God for their national security. They failed to execute justice in their courts. They failed to care for the poor and needy among their people. They failed to steer clear of all other gods and their respective worship practices. They domesticated Israel's priests, divested the tribes of equal status, and subsumed all power and authority under one human head: the king.

They came out from Babylon and Egypt only to become a smaller and weaker version of them. There was nothing impressive about that. They were not shining a distinctive light. When looking at Israel, neighboring nations could only appreciate their own image being reflected back at them. The Israelites neither blessed the nations nor rendered priestly service on their behalf. Instead, they conducted international business as usual.

Through the prophets, God gave his people a piece of his mind. They detailed every destructive misdemeanor and cast every vision of a wholesome alternative. Yet they never fault God's people for neglecting to make the world a better place. They never lament Israel's failure to use its temporary success and fleeting wealth to improve the lives of weaker and poorer peoples to the north, south, east, and west. Though eighth-century prophets like Amos, Hosea, Micah, and Isaiah decried all manner of social injustice being perpetrated by one Israelite upon another, there were no such warnings for *not* reaching out into foreign lands to lend a helping hand.[1]

The Israelites were never rebuked for ignoring the widows and orphans of neighboring nations because Torah never asked them to see

---

1. Jonah is no exception. God did not send him to Nineveh to impart information from Torah that would make Assyria a better place. Jonah's only mission was to announce that God planned to destroy the capital city. After Jonah reluctantly made that announcement, the pagan king takes the initiative to call for repentance and initiate all the reforms that followed (Jonah 3:6–9). The *Assyrian* powers carry out all the reforms.

to their needs. Torah's vision called them to care only for the poor and needy members of their own community (Deut 15).

Though they were asked to care for strangers passing through their land and for aliens taking refuge on their property, such hospitality was a necessary extension of their life together. There could only be one rule for all people in the land (Exod 12:49; Lev 24:19). Exceptions could not be tolerated. That would create a two-tiered ethic that would eventually compromise the integrity of Israel's witness. Such kindness to strangers was never viewed as a strategy for improving the world; it was a function of self-preservation. It was not an initial foray into ruling over the nations, but a deliberate means of keeping the rules of the nations from seeping into their own land.

The only dominion mandate implied in Torah and the prophets is the mandate to rule over their own land on loan from God according to specific instructions. God never authorized them to rule over people or places beyond the promised land. Though some of Israel's most powerful kings did this on a limited scale for a limited time, it did not and could not last without compromising the blessing that God was forming Israel to be.

The Israelites disregarded the prophets, so God removed the kingship from them, as well as territorial sovereignty and national independence. Since they did not use their land for God's purpose, God gave it to others to look after. He gave it first to Assyria, then Babylon, and eventually Persia. By the time of Jesus, it passed through the hands of the Greeks and Romans as well.

Hope for a Better Place

Still, God's prophets had not given up all hope. They firmly believed that God would remember his creation. *Somehow, some way, God would intervene decisively in world history. God would step in and make this world a better place.* When he does, wars will end. People will live long abundant lives. Creation will be restored from the curse. Humans and animals, predators and prey, will live in harmony with one another. God will pour his Spirit upon all people, and all nations will embrace his reign.[2]

But first God will have to remember his chosen people. He will send his Messiah who will gather them from among the nations. He will renew

---

2. Isa 2:1–4; 65:17–25; Ezek 47:9–12; Joel 2:28–29; Mic 4:1–4.

his covenant with them and write his laws upon their hearts. Only then will they resume their priestly vocation and become a light to all nations. Only then will all nations be blessed through them. Only then will all creation be wrapped up in God's ultimate plan to redeem and restore all things.[3]

This world will become a better place, but God's people must first become the better place that God called them to be on behalf of this world.

---

3. Isa 35:1–10; 42:1–9; Jer 31:31–34; Amos 9:11–5; Mic 4:1–2.

8

God Sends Jesus to Inaugurate a Better Place, Part I

Preparing the Way

"ARE YOU THE ONE who is to come, or are we to wait for another?" (Matt 11:3).

This was a logical question. It was *the* question to ask. John the Baptist had dedicated his adult life to proclaiming that God's kingdom was near (Matt 3:2). And he didn't just proclaim it—he lived it. He enacted it in diet, deed, and dress. Now he was paying the ultimate price for it: life in prison. Ultimately, it was a death sentence. The Baptist held nothing back. Jesus called him the greatest man who ever lived (11:11).

Why such high praise? The answer is simple. John did not live for himself. Everything he did was for the kingdom. It was his life's obsession, and it cost him dearly. So as his body wasted away in prison, he couldn't help but wonder, "Was it all worth it?"

Was everything he lived for—and would soon die for—coming to pass as he expected? Was the kingdom of God truly at hand? Was Jesus truly the king?

John didn't choose this calling; he was born into it. His father was a priest. His mother bore him by miracle. He was filled with God's Spirit while still in the womb (Luke 1:15). His destiny was announced in advance by the angel Gabriel: "to make ready *a people* prepared for the Lord" (v. 17). God was coming, and this meant that everything was going to change. The hope of the prophets was bursting forth into reality. God was coming for his world, which meant he was coming first for his people.

Kingdom Come

John poses his questions to Jesus, and Jesus' answer is clear: the blind see, the lame walk, the deaf hear, lepers are cleansed, the dead live, and the poor receive good news (Matt 11:4–6). What's more, all who embrace the new reality made possible by Jesus become greater than John the Baptist, the greatest man who ever lived (v. 11).

The kingdom preached, people prepared, signs performed—the new era in world history that the prophet's foretold had begun. Jesus had inaugurated God's kingdom. Like elected presidents delivering their inaugural address, Jesus signaled the beginning of his time in office. In his case, however, there were no term limits; it was a time that would never end. Scripture uses a variety of terms to describe what was happening:

Salvation	Fullness of time	End of ages
Redemption	New era	End of days
Restoration	New creation	Day of the Lord
Reconciliation	New age	Year of the Lord
Renewal	New life	Times of refreshing
Fulfillment	Eternal life	Kingdom of heaven

As far as we can tell, Jesus most often used the phrase "kingdom of God" to describe what God was doing through him. This phrase has gone in and out of style over the years. It has been used to describe a variety of competing ideas. In fact, it is used to support each of the Christian approaches to a better place discussed in Part One.

Preachers committed to using plain language often avoid kingdom talk. This is understandable but regrettable, since they don't generally come up with good substitutes. More often than not, they use other terms that also have to be heavily defined before they can be properly understood—terms like *salvation, gospel, grace, eternal life,* and *heaven.* They tend to sidestep political jargon like *empire, dominion, nation, country, commonwealth, province, realm,* and *revolution.*

The problem with much of the available language is that we need words that will do for us what the phrase *kingdom of God* did for the original hearers. We need words that say, "Jesus came to do what the prophets of Israel said God was going to do through his people under the leadership of God's appointed ruler." That's a lot to look for in a phrase!

Kingdom language worked for Jesus because he used it among a community with a shared tradition. First-century Jews weren't unique in this. To be on an athletic team today you need to learn new vocabulary. Tennis players need to know that "love" means zero points. Baseball players need to know that "stealing" a base means running to where it is, not taking it with you. Various trades also use in-house language. When painters speak of "cutting in" a room, they don't mean slicing something with a sharp instrument, but rather painting in and around the edges and corners. The term "deadhead" likewise connotes quite different things to truckers, gardeners, plumbers, and classic rock fans.

It should not surprise us, then, that joining the people of God might require learning technical terms. Until accurate nontechnical language becomes available, I suggest we use kingdom language and find a helpful way to explain what it means—without diluting its core substance. The Gospels provide a way forward by introducing the kingdom as "good news." Even this term had political overtones in Jesus' day that are often lost on us today, but it still serves us well.

In grade school English, many of us were taught how to report news. To tell the whole story, an author must answer the five Ws (and one H): who, what, when, where, why, and how. Who was involved? What happened? When did it happen? Where did it happen? Why did it happen? How did it happen?

Since the gospel is quite literally *news* and because this journalistic formula is common knowledge today, it serves as a convenient device for reporting the news of God's kingdom. I take two chapters to answer these six questions. For my purposes, the *who* and *how* require the most explanation. The remaining four Ws between them require less because they have been addressed earlier in the Bible story.

Who is Involved in God's Kingdom?

As with most kingdoms, God's kingdom has both rulers and the ruled. The king is God Most High, and his son Jesus reigns at his right hand. The God of Abraham entrusted all power in heaven and on earth to Jesus (Matt 28:18). Jesus wasn't an ordinary, run-of-the-mill ruler. He was the king for whom Israel was waiting—the Messiah who was appointed to restore the fortunes of Israel. He was the one who would renew God's blessing upon Israel and then bless all nations through Israel.

The ruled, then, are those who submit to God's reign through Jesus. Kingdom people seek first God's kingdom. We learn in the New Testament that God's kingdom began with Israel. In fact, Jesus explicitly states that he was sent only to the "lost sheep of Israel" (Matt 15:24). This is not because God doesn't care about other people. It is because Jesus refused to do Israel's job for Israel. God promised that he would use Abraham's descendants to bless all nations. He didn't send Jesus to break that promise, but to fulfill it.

Peter says as much in one of the first gospel sermons preached to the Jews after the ascension of Jesus: "You are the descendants of the prophets and of the covenant that God gave to your ancestors, saying to Abraham, 'And in your descendants all the families of the earth shall be blessed.' When God raised up his servant, he sent him first to you, to bless you by turning each of you from your wicked ways" (Acts 3:25–26).

God did not intend for Israel to always have the exclusive right to be his kingdom people. To the surprise of many, he incorporates other ethnic groups into Israel in a way that changes the rules concerning those who are and are not God's people. What results is nothing less than a new humanity:

> But now in Christ Jesus you who once were far off have been brought near by the blood of Christ. For he is our peace; in his flesh he has made both groups [Jews and non-Jews] into one and has broken down the dividing wall, that is, the hostility between us. He has abolished the law with its commandments and ordinances, that he might create in himself one new humanity in place of the two, thus making peace, and might reconcile both groups to God in one body through the cross, thus putting to death that hostility through it. (Eph 2:13–16)

The kingdom has a people. It has its own specific citizenry (Phil 3:20). It is a "chosen race, a royal priesthood, a holy nation, God's own people" (1 Pet 2:9). In our day, it has become fashionable to separate the people of God from the kingdom of God and to speak as if God's kingdom work happens wherever God's justice breaks forth in this world. In fact, some people even use the phrase "church centered" to discuss what happens among the local body of Christ and "kingdom centered" to describe whatever good is done outside of the body.[1]

---

1. See McNeal, *Kingdom Come*.

To speak this way is unbiblical. The local body of believers is God's kingdom work. We don't *do* that work; we *are* that work! God is building a kingdom, Jesus is the cornerstone, and his people are the building (1 Pet 2:4–9; Eph 2:19–22; 1 Cor 3:9–17). We are the people who submit to the king and seek first his kingdom. We are not a private, insular kingdom. The king wishes to expand the scope of his realm and to welcome as many people into it as possible.

People routinely point out that Jesus never planted a church. They usually deduce from this that he was all about the kingdom and *not* the church. They miss out on one critical fact: Jesus didn't have to start a church because God already had a community of faith. He had Israel. They were his people. Jesus was committed first and foremost to gathering and revitalizing that particular faith community.

It is undeniably true that no one was more committed to God's kingdom than Jesus, and it is equally true that no one was more committed to the community of faith than Jesus. This should be our first clue that commitment to one cannot be separated from commitment to the other. Though one can be committed to church life and church programming in ways that miss out on God's kingdom reality, one cannot be committed to God's kingdom work without being committed to the body of Christ.

Of course, God still works wonders outside the body of Christ. But this is nothing new. God has been working through the kingdoms of this world to create conditions in which all humans may thrive since the time of Babel. The Gospel of Matthew refers to God's kingdom as the "kingdom *of heaven*" in order to distinguish it from the kingdoms of this world.[2] Though many have noted that God rules over all creation, no Israelite prophet, priest, or king ever referred to God's work among the nations as his "kingdom work." Rather, it is God's work as creator and sustainer to preserve his creation and look after all creatures.

That work did not begin anew in Jesus. It has been going on without interruption since primeval times. God could use anyone to do it. No one has to repent before entering into that work. New birth and the Holy Spirit are not necessary. It is God's pleasure to continue that work for the sake of his broken world despite human rebellion. Disciples of Jesus are not called *specifically* to that work, but there is a long line of willing unbelievers who are eager to dedicate their lives to it.

---

2. See Pennington, *Heaven and Earth in the Gospel of Matthew.*

There are biblical-sounding reasons why someone might equate God's providential work in the world with his kingdom work. After all, the Lord's Prayer says, "Your kingdom come. Your will be done, on earth as it is in heaven" (Matt 6:10). It only takes a small step to deduce from this that wherever and whenever God's will is done, the kingdom is coming. But this is too simple and does not take the context seriously.

Right before this line, Jesus prays, "Hallowed be thy name" (v. 9). This phrase is not a generic way of saying something nice about God. In the original language it is a soft "command," as are the following lines.[3] Using the soft command form doesn't mean that the speaker exercises authority over the person to whom he or she is speaking. It's simply how certain languages signal a request. In this prayer, Jesus is literally asking God to sanctify his name, to bring his kingdom, and to do his will. For God to sanctify his name—to make it holy—is to restore Israel so that through its witness the nations may see God's glory.

This interpretation is more apparent when we consider its origin in the prophecy of Ezekiel:

> Therefore say to the house of Israel, Thus says the Lord GOD: It is not for your sake, O house of Israel, that I am about to act, but for the sake of my holy name, which you have profaned among the nations to which you came. I will sanctify my great name, which has been profaned among the nations, and which you have profaned among them; and the nations shall know that I am the LORD, says the Lord GOD, when through you I display my holiness before their eyes. I will take you from the nations, and gather you from all the countries, and bring you into your own land. (Ezek 36:22–24)

This is another way of saying what we have been saying all along. God's saving intention is to use Abraham's descendants to bless all nations. God will bless his people and then use their blessed status to attract the nations. By Ezekiel's time, God had begun to bless the Israelites, but they rejected that blessing. So the opposite happened. Instead of drawing the nations to their holy God, they disgraced God's holy name among the nations. God then disgraced the Israelites by removing his blessing from them and allowing the nations to have their way with them. Yet Ezekiel clarifies that this was only temporary. There will come a day when God

---

3. For a helpful discussion of this passage, see Lohfink, *Jesus and Community*, 14–17.

sanctifies his name by gathering and blessing his people so that they, in turn, may be a blessing to the nations.

In Jesus, that day had come. God was doing his will by restoring his people so they may glorify his name among the nations. The kingdom work of Jesus was God's work among Israel on behalf of all people. It was not God's work among all people independent of his people.

The kingdom indeed has a people and—like it or not—it's us.[4]

What is God's Kingdom?

Answering the *what* of God's kingdom is perhaps the trickiest part. The first thing we can be sure of is that it was a fulfillment of Israel's expectations. This is most important. The gospel was not presented as generic news that answers wider humanity's sense of longing. It was the specific fulfillment of a specific people's expectations.

Jesus' mother was a poor Jewish woman who knew what it meant when the angel spoke to her. When told that she was carrying a child whose kingdom would not end, Mary did not ask *what* the kingdom was, she only asked *how* it could be, since she was a virgin (Luke 1:34). After embracing this possibility, she broke out in song about the God who has shown mercy to generations of his people by scattering the proud, bringing down the powerful, filling the hungry, impoverishing the rich, and remembering his promises to Abraham and his descendants.

Mary's kin also knew what the kingdom meant. When her cousin Elizabeth gave birth to John the Baptist—who was appointed to prepare the way for the kingdom—her husband Zechariah also broke out in song. He blessed the God of Israel for redeeming his people, raising up a savior from the house of David, fulfilling the words of the prophets, rescuing Israel from all enemies, remembering his covenant, and keeping his oath to Abraham (Luke 1:67–79). Indeed, if there is one thing clear about the *what* of the kingdom, it's that whatever it was, it fulfilled Israel's expectations.

Things become more complicated when we turn to the second thing we know about God's kingdom: that it didn't fulfill Israel's expectations the way that many Jews had expected. This is where a lot of confusion and speculation comes from. If the kingdom wasn't what the Jews expected,

---

4. McKnight's *Kingdom Conspiracy* stands out among recent books for emphasizing the connection between God's kingdom and the church.

maybe it was something totally different. Instead of looking to the prophets and saying, "It is this," we are tempted to say, "It must *not* be this." After all, that is what the Jews expected, and they turned out to be wrong.

This logic has led readers to focus on what Jesus' followers *didn't* understand about the kingdom. Jesus rebuked his disciples on several occasions for wanting to know who would be greatest in the kingdom, who would sit on the left and right side of his throne. Jesus also redirected them whenever they hinted at taking over Jerusalem and setting up a new regime. Many have deduced from this that the disciples' expectations were too political and too earthly. As a result, more spiritual and heavenly versions of the kingdom soon began to replace them.

This is entirely understandable, but it still misses the mark. It focuses on when Jesus' followers got it wrong and then bases its alternative on the opposite of what they thought. That is no way to define anything accurately. We should focus instead on the instances when the disciples got it right. When did the kingdom finally click for them? When did they get it so thoroughly that from that point forward they couldn't help but joyfully proclaim it?

Like Mary and Zechariah, many of the disciples grasped the big picture early on. How else was Jesus able to send them out in pairs to proclaim the kingdom? When they returned and reported back to him, he declared their mission a success (Luke 10). How could they succeed if they had no idea what they were talking about? They must have understood it well enough to speak successfully about it.

Even so, their understanding was incomplete. Even after Jesus rose from the dead they asked him, "Is this the time when you will restore the kingdom to Israel?" (Acts 1:6). They were still eager to storm Jerusalem, oust the Romans, and place Jesus on the throne. Jesus' response is telling. He instructs them, in essence, to stop looking at their "watches" and to bear witness to all that they had seen and heard (vv. 6–8).

Then something happens that changes everything. Jesus ascends into heaven before their very eyes. Amazed and overjoyed, the disciples spring into action. They return to Jerusalem, replace Judas, receive the spirit, and begin preaching the kingdom.[5] Luke's gospel adds that immediately

---

5. The disciples' insistence on replacing Judas should not be overlooked. They realized that Jesus chose twelve disciples for a reason. This group of twelve represents God's restoration of Israel. God promised first to restore his people, then fill them with his Spirit, and then make them a light to the nations. Because the disciples saw themselves as continuing Israel's mission, it was crucial for them to replace Judas. They

following the ascension they worshiped him, returned to Jerusalem with great joy, and continually blessed God in the temple (24:52–53).

The ascension changed everything. When Jesus left his followers behind and assumed his rightful place at the Father's right hand, then and only then did the kingdom finally click for them. You see, the disciples were not wrong to expect Jesus to establish a political kingdom on earth. Their earlier vision wasn't too political or too earthly; it was too *small*. God's kingdom doesn't exclude politics or the earth; it simply places them within a wider frame.

The disciples wanted a king in Jerusalem who would rule over all of Israel. Jesus could never accept that. Again, it was just too small a kingdom. Satan made a similar offer at the beginning of Jesus' ministry (Matt 4). But Jesus was no mere national king. His reign could not be contained by a tiny plot of land in Palestine. His reign couldn't even be contained by the larger territory of the Roman Empire. The Apostle Paul makes this clear, saying, "God put this power to work in Christ when he raised him from the dead and seated him at his right hand in the heavenly realms, far above all rule and authority, power and dominion, and every title that can be given, not only in the present age but also in the one to come" (Eph 1:20–21).

The ascension placed all of the disciples' misunderstandings into perspective. With Jesus seated at God's right hand, it seemed silly to ask where *they* might sit. With Jesus in command of the cosmos, it made sense why a local coup in Palestine was out of place. With God's power on full display, horses, chariots, and swords no longer seemed all that helpful. After the ascension, the disciples finally realized that *they* were not going to bring the kingdom at all. God had already brought the kingdom through Jesus and their primary role was to bear witness to this fact.

What, then, is the kingdom? It is the fulfillment of Israel's hopes. It is the reign of God over his people on behalf of all creation. It is the new world order that the prophets foretold. It is everything God's people longed for, and more. It is Israel's God intervening in world history to make a better place in this world.

---

wanted it to be clear to all people that they were not starting a new religion but carrying forward the legacy of Abraham, Moses, and Jacob's twelve sons.

9

God Sends Jesus to Inaugurate a Better Place, Part II

Where is God's Kingdom?

IN MANY WAYS WE have already identified the *where* of God's kingdom. The Bible story begins with the fall of physical creation. What God had made good, humans wrecked. It recounts how God intervened to rescue this world from the brink of destruction by cleansing it of nearly all life. But then God promises never to destroy this world again (Gen 8:20–22). He commits to finding some other way to deal with human corruption. That other way begins with Abraham.

Since Abraham, the biblical hope has been that God would redeem and restore *this* world. Abraham anticipated that his descendants would be a blessing to all the earth's families. The prophets foretold a day when peace would prevail among all creatures, when the soil would give forth its fruit liberally, and when Jerusalem would ring with songs of joy (Isa 2:1–4; 65:17–25). The book of Daniel envisions a day when the kingdoms of this earth are supplanted by God's kingdom *here on earth* (chs. 2, 7).

No Old Testament passage suggests that God's people may someday leave this earth and go to heaven or anywhere else. Though Enoch walked with God and was no more, and Elijah disappeared into the clouds never to be seen again, we are never told where they went. Even if we were to assume they went to heaven—against the testimony of Jesus (John 3:13)—the Scriptures never suggest that other people would follow their lead. These men were puzzling exceptions that led Jews to speculate as to what special purpose God might have for them.[1]

The New Testament picks up where the Old Testament leaves off. In the Beatitudes, Jesus speaks of the meek inheriting *the earth*. In the Lord's Prayer, he speaks of the kingdom in terms of God's will being done *on earth* as it is in heaven. When speaking of the gospel, Jesus emphasizes that the kingdom has come near (Matt 4:17; 10:7) and is among God's people (Luke 17:20–21).

Paul speaks of creation groaning to be restored in Romans 8. Multiple passages speak about the reconciliation and restoration of all things (Matt 17:11; Acts 3:21; Col 1:20). Nowhere does the Bible depict God abandoning his creation. Revelation 21 echoes the language of Isaiah to affirm a new heavens and earth—not in terms of replacing them but in terms of renewing and restoring them. Revelation leaves us with the picture of a New Jerusalem coming *down out of heaven* (vv. 2, 10) and resting upon the earth.

Though a few phrases scattered throughout the Bible could be misread to suggest an otherworldly view of the kingdom, the basic plot line of Scripture runs sharply against it.[2] This is not to deny that Christ's influence extends beyond this earth. "On earth *as it is in heaven*" implies a correlation between God's reign on earth and in heaven (Matt 6:10). New Testament passages extolling the grandeur of Christ also emphasize his lordship over the entire cosmos, including all creatures both earthly and heavenly (Eph 1; Col 1).

As pertains to humans, however, Scripture's hope revolves around a kingdom that encompasses this earth. It may extend beyond earth, but it never leaves earth behind. It may involve a dramatic change of affairs on earth, such that metaphors of destruction are fitting (2 Pet 3:7–12), but the end result is not the abandonment but the refinement of this world.

1. This is why we see a flurry of Enoch literature produced during the intertestamental period—most notably 1 Enoch, which is quoted in Jude 14–15. Elijah, on the other hand, was expected to return to God's people somehow. This is evident in Malachi 4:5 and the later Jewish practice of leaving an empty seat for Elijah at the annual Passover Seder.

2. See Middleton, *A New Heaven and a New Earth*; Snyder, *Salvation Means Creation Healed*; and Wright, *Surprised by Hope*.

When is God's Kingdom?

The classic way to express the *when* of God's kingdom is to say that it is "already but not yet." This phrase captures the New Testament's teaching that Jesus truly inaugurated God's kingdom here on earth, but did not bring it completely. Some of Israel's hopes have been fulfilled, but not all.

For instance, God has already kept his promises to send the Messiah, make a new covenant, pour out his Spirit, and send his people out as a blessing to all nations. But still our bodies continue to suffer corruption, creation groans to be restored, lives are cut short, wickedness thrives, oppression continues, and the dead are not raised. It's not that God hasn't done anything. Tremendous things have happened. But, surely not *everything* has happened.

The church's tendency has been to emphasize the "not yet" at the expense of the "already." The not yet has caused many, even Jesus' forerunner John the Baptist, to question the already. The prophets did not foresee that the Messiah would first begin the kingdom and much later complete the kingdom. This sort of innovation seems suspicious. It's a pretty big detail for the prophets to leave out.

On another level, something like this is exactly what God's promise to Abraham required. Had Jesus brought the kingdom all at once, he would have had to gather Israel, raise the dead, judge all people, bring low the nations, vanquish all evil, restore creation, and somehow simultaneously use his people as a blessing to all nations.

This diverse list presents some logistical problems if one were attempting to fulfill them all at once. Who would have been worthy to survive God's judgment? Romans 1 tells us that both Jews and Gentiles stand condemned before God. Had the wicked been vanquished in the first coming of Christ, few, if any, would have remained to populate God's new creation.

Perhaps most importantly, a window of time needed to be created for Jewish witness to the Gentiles. The Old Testament reveals both that Israel needed to be saved and that God's people must fulfill their calling to be a light to the nations. The world needed time—time for the nations to stream to Jerusalem or, as it turned out, time for God's word to go forth from Jerusalem to the nations (Luke 24:47).

The prophets anticipated that the Messiah would gather God's people *and* that the gathered people would bless all nations. They must have also known this would take time. The Messiah's kingdom work must begin at one point and would not reach fulfillment until much later. Peter links Christ's delay with evangelism, saying "The Lord is not slow about his promise, as some think of slowness, but is patient with you, not wanting any to perish, but all to come to repentance" (2 Pet 3:9).

This raises the question of why Jesus brought the kingdom at all during his first coming. Why not gather, equip, and send Israel to the nations and return later to bring the full kingdom all at once? This leads to the *how* of God's kingdom, which I discuss below—after briefly addressing the *why*.

Why was God's Kingdom Needed?

We've discussed the *why* of God's kingdom in previous chapters. The *why* of God's kingdom is, essentially, the Bible story up until this point. Human sin made a mess of God's world, but God loved this world enough not to abandon it to self-destruction. So he took preventative measures to limit the damage humans might do to one another and creation. Then God formed a people from Abraham's descendants through whom he would bless all nations. He worked patiently with this people as he shaped them for their mission.

This process had its ups and downs, as one might expect with people. The Israelites complicated things considerably by forsaking God's covenant and conforming their life to the image of surrounding nations. This detour brought a good deal of heartache to God and his people. In loving discipline, God withdrew his protection and allowed stronger nations to break Israel apart.

Still God did not give up on his people. He promised to forgive their sins, send them a ruler who would gather them from among the nations, and renew his covenant with them. Restoring Israel was not an end in itself. It was vital to God's blessing of all nations. It was part of God's wider goal of leading all creation out of bondage and into the fullness of glory that he has in store. At the end of the day, then, God's kingdom was needed in order to fulfill God's original purposes for all creation.

How does God's Kingdom Come?

How does God's kingdom come? *It comes as a gift.*

God had plenty of resources at his disposal to inaugurate his kingdom. He could have appointed a special Israelite to do so, like John the Baptist. He could have converted and made use of a powerful nation. He could have sent 10,000 angels to clean up this world and make it a better place. But he didn't.

Instead, God sent his Son, who became flesh and walked among us. It was a strange thing to do. No one saw it coming. Still, it made sense. God has always wanted a people who would accept his reign over them as a gift. Any other way into his kingdom would be just another form of subjugation. A mighty kingdom like Rome cannot offer their regime as a gift. Their military strength forces subjects into compliance. A battalion of heavenly angels would have a similar effect. Who could resist them?

Since God's reign is a gift, he offers it in a form that is rejectable. World kingdoms have a steady track record of making offers people cannot refuse. When they take over a new territory, it looks and feels more like organized crime. Sure, there are benefits, but the new loyalty they command is forced. God's better world doesn't come like that because it is fundamentally unlike that.

How could an almighty God offer a rejectable kingdom? How could he do so in such a way that his awesome presence doesn't hover over the offering and smother the will of the recipients? God's answer has always been to make his offer through a lowly people. He accomplishes it by his power, and his lowly people announce the good news to the nations.

God therefore sent Jesus to his lowly people. Jesus walked among the lowest of them as one of them. From that posture, he announced and demonstrated the new reality of God's kingdom. He revealed that God wasn't finished with his people; he was saving them. He forgives their sins, lifts their heads, and focuses their vision for global mission.

Yet God's people didn't have the best track record. They often misrepresented God by rejecting his way of life and embracing the ways of the nations. With Jesus, things were different. As long as he was with them, they could see clearly. As long as he was triumphing over their enemies, they could trust God's power. With him in their midst, God's kingdom was indeed at hand. They could see it, feel it, and even taste it in the breaking of bread. Jesus radiated God's goodness.

It's no wonder the disciples balked at the notion that Jesus might die and leave them stranded. How could they hold it together? He was their glue. Aware of their frailty, Jesus comforted them. He vowed not to leave them as orphans. He would send them his Spirit. The Spirit would guide them into truth. It would act powerfully through and among them. All power in heaven and earth had been given to Jesus, and he gave a portion of that power to his people.

The gift of the Holy Spirit is not like coercive human power. It is not the irresistible force of horses and chariots, of drones and stealth bombers. It is a gift that can be rejected. It is power that can be resisted. It can be quenched. It can be denied. Remember the bystanders on Pentecost who accused the apostles of being drunk. The Spirit doesn't have to get its way in our lives—or else! It would rather move on than mow over stubborn humans.

This is not to say that God's Spirit could not force our compliance or that there aren't negative consequences for resisting God's Spirit.[3] It is only to say that this is not how God chooses his Spirit to work routinely in the lives of believers. For God's Spirit to show itself continually in obvious ways that are immune to misinterpretation and rejection is to deny the possibility of human faith. Who could say "no" to an ever-present flurry of undeniable miracles?

God knew that not all humans would accept the gift of his kingdom. He knew that rebellious powers would feel threatened by a regime that they couldn't understand or control because it didn't play by their rules. But God's gift was total. He was prepared to go all the way with his resistible gift. That could only mean one thing in the first century: the cross.

God does not lovingly offer his kingdom until it meets resistance and then back away, switch approaches, and force people to comply. God is not like us. Rather than overwhelm us with his sovereign might, he sent Jesus in the flesh.

In the flesh, the power at work in Jesus could only be in one place at a time. Yet God's kingdom could not be tied permanently to Jesus' flesh. So God handed that flesh over to the powers and principalities. In doing so, he exposed their power for what it truly is. The powers do not serve God like he created them to. The authorities don't consistently punish the wicked and reward the good. They reward whatever pads their pockets and strengthens their rule. They punish whatever threatens their power. They punish the one who inaugurates a better kingdom.

Their usual tactics didn't work on Jesus. They couldn't coerce a retraction out of him. Their smooth-talking politicians couldn't manipulate him into backing down from threatening claims. Jesus knew that any

3. Those who blaspheme against the Holy Spirit are not forgiven (Matt 12:21) and some have died for lying to the Holy Spirit (Acts 5:1–10).

power they had was on loan from God (John 19:11) and that God would soon hand all power over to him.

There was only one trick left in their bag. It was a last resort, but it guaranteed results: death by crucifixion. It was brutal and public. It stood as a stern warning to every passerby. This is what happens to enemies of the existing regime. This is what they do to champions of a better world that is different from the one they are offering. The powers respond by killing the Messiah.

The results were predictable. Jesus' followers fled. They went home in defeat. How could they have been so easily duped? How gullible to think they were forerunners of a better world. Their parents were right. The religious establishment was right. What were they thinking? They were nobodies, mere fisherman, women of little account. Nothing good comes from Nazareth after all.

And then the brilliance of God's plan became apparent. God's better world does not come from Nazareth; it comes from the power of resurrection. In raising Jesus from the dead, God communicates with unmistakable clarity that his kingdom does not come through human effort. It is a divine accomplishment from start to finish.

It was God who gave a son to childless Abraham and Sarah, God who brought Israel out of Egypt, God who entrusted the land of Canaan to his people, God who held powerful empires at bay, God who led the Israelites into exile and back out. It was God who sent the Messiah, inaugurated the kingdom, and allowed the powers to do everything they could to stop it. It was God who raised the Messiah from the grave, seated him on high, and sent his Spirit to empower the witness of his people in this world.

It is not us. It was never supposed to be us. It is natural for us to assume that it's our job. Since we made a mess of this world, we should clean it up. We call this responsibility. But we're not in charge of this world. We don't get to make the rules. God claims responsibility for his creation, and he has taken initiative to restore it.

God's people still have an important role. He didn't create us for nothing. But our role is not to fix the world for God. Our role, by the power of God's Spirit, is to bear faithful witness to God's saving work on creation's behalf.

Notice how Scripture depicts the gift of God's Spirit. God did not give us his Spirit to empower us to change the world. His power doesn't enable us to be more persuasive politicians, more influential Ivy League educators, more strategic military commanders, more entertaining cultural trendsetters, more innovative inventors, or more benevolent philanthropists. In chapter 1, we noted Hunter's findings that this is the kind of power that brings lasting change in this world. Yet we find no such power among God's people in the New Testament.

God gave us his Spirit so we might testify boldly about what God has done. He gave us the Spirit so the church would have everything it needs to display God's kingdom in our unassuming life together. The Spirit moves us to embrace God's kingdom, display God's kingdom, and proclaim God's kingdom throughout the world. God sent Jesus in the flesh so that the kingdom's true nature could be revealed, so that we might know that we have a choice. We can reject God's offer. And yet God still moves. In the flesh, Jesus could only be in one place at a time. In the Spirit, Christ's body bears witness to his accomplished work all throughout the world, all at the same time.

The Apostle Paul succinctly states how God's kingdom comes: "So if anyone is in Christ, there is a new creation: everything old has passed away; see, everything has become new! All this is from God, who reconciled us to himself through Christ, and has given us the ministry of reconciliation; that is, in Christ God was reconciling the world to himself, not counting their trespasses against them, and entrusting the message of reconciliation to us" (2 Cor 5:17–19).

God's kingdom has come in Jesus. Everything old is passing. Everything has become new. There is a new creation. But most importantly, for our purposes, "All this is *from God*"! It is God who reconciled us and God who reconciled the world to himself. He is the one who made all things new. All of this is an accomplished fact. As Jesus declared on the cross, "It is finished" (John 19:3). That work is complete, and we didn't lift a finger to complete it. Our ministry is to spread the news, the *good* news of God's kingdom.

God's Kingdom and a Better Place

I have spent time unpacking the nature of God's kingdom because it is central to Scripture's vision of a better place. One does not arrive at a biblical vision by looking at this broken world and dreaming up an alternative that is more to our liking. That is the path to idolatry. It leads to human-concocted utopias.

We end up imagining that a better place is other-worldly, when it is very much this worldly. We end up imagining that a better place is entirely future, when it has already begun. We end up imagining that we are the change agents who make this world better, when God claims full responsibility for doing so.

With a clearer picture of God's kingdom in mind, we are better positioned to discern the precise role of God's people in God's plan for a better place.

10

God Calls the Church to Embrace a Better Place

INCOMPLETE VISIONS OF A better place—the heaven-centered, human-centered, and world-centered views we looked at in chapter 2—falter for all kinds of different reasons. They hold in common a tendency to distort or diminish the role of God's people. By relocating the better place beyond the clouds, the heaven-centered view reduces the church to a ticket-punching agency and holding station. By mistaking who makes this world a better place, the human-centered view authorizes the church to do work that God has not prepared us to do and that we don't do particularly well. And by not making a clear distinction between nonhuman creation and God's new creation people, the world-centered view diminishes the significance of God's people as the forerunners of God's new creation and softens its implications for our life together.

In the previous chapter, I discussed how God brought his kingdom about through Jesus. I quoted 2 Corinthians 5:17–19 and emphasized that the new creation is God's doing and not ours. A better place is not our work to do; it is our gift to receive. But God has called the church to be more than passive recipients. To get at this *more* we need to keep reading this passage and see where Paul goes with it:

> If anyone is in Christ, there is a new creation: everything old has passed away; see, everything has become new! All this is from God, who reconciled us to himself through Christ, and has given us the ministry of reconciliation; that is, in Christ God was reconciling the world to himself, not counting their trespasses against them, and entrusting the message of reconciliation to us. So we are ambassadors for Christ, since God is making his

77

> appeal through us; we entreat you on behalf of Christ, be recon-
> ciled to God. For our sake he made him to be sin who knew no
> sin, so that in him we might become the righteousness of God.
> (2 Cor 5:17–21)

Though God accomplished the work of inaugurating a new creation and reconciling this world to himself, he makes his appeal to the world *through us*. He has appointed us his ambassadors. He has no other strategy. If we don't represent him before the world, the world will not know that it has been reconciled to God. It's already a done deal, but it needs messengers who will proclaim the good news (Rom 10:14–15).

The image of ambassadors is rich in meaning. Ambassadors are citizens of one kingdom who represent their government to citizens of other kingdoms. America has ambassadors in various countries throughout the world. These ambassadors live abroad, but they represent America. Even on foreign soil, they live in embassies among fellow Americans. Their ultimate allegiance to the United States is transparent to their host countries. Their hosts don't begrudge them this. They, too, have ambassadors who represent them throughout the world.

According to this passage, God has already revealed a better world, a new creation. Christians are its citizens. We have already entered it. But creation isn't *new* for everyone. It is only new to those who are in Christ. The present form of this world is passing away, but most people are oblivious to it (1 Cor 7:31). That is why God calls us to declare and represent his better world to others. Even though God sits enthroned over all nations and works among each one, he does not claim them as his kingdom. His kingdom is still a minority movement in this world. We are its ambassadors. Rival kingdoms, even hostile ones, still exist.

As far as God is concerned, he has absorbed and conquered all hostility in Christ (Eph 2:16). He has brokered a lasting peace. God's kingdom will indeed envelop all kingdoms and encompass all territories, but he will neither force them into it nor count them as default citizens of it. Instead, he appeals to them through meek and vulnerable ambassadors whose claims are debatable and whose offer can be rejected (2 Cor 4:7–10).

As ambassadors, the church represents the better place of God's kingdom in three ways. We must embrace God's kingdom, display God's kingdom, and proclaim God's kingdom.

Embracing God's Kingdom

Embracing God's kingdom means more than saying, "Yes, I want to be part of God's new world." It means truly believing that God, in Christ, has made this world new. God's new world is not readily apparent to unbelievers. This is why Paul says, "*If anyone is in Christ*, there is a new creation: everything old has passed away; see, everything has become new" (2 Cor 5:17).

This new creation is not some mystical, invisible, disembodied reality. God's new creation has taken preliminary form in the body of Christ. We are the new world on the way. We are as much of the new order as anyone or anything is currently able to see or experience.

This is why Romans 8 depicts nonhuman creation as longing for the revealing of God's children who possess the first fruits of God's Spirit. It's why Ephesians 2 speaks of the church as a new humanity, God's holy temple, God's dwelling place. It's why Galatians 6 refers to God's people as new creation. It's why Hebrews 4 speaks of Christians as having already entered into God's rest.

These passages are certainly not referring to the church's current experience of the wider world. They are speaking of the dramatically new life that believers now live in Christ and in fellowship with one another.

The Church and God's Better World

I have spoken of the church in our day in more exalted terms than Christians generally do. But I have not done so any more than the New Testament does. To bring home this point as clearly as possible, I have gathered together under seven headings numerous New Testament statements that testify to the new and better world that God's people have already entered through Christ. Their collective force is humbling and sobering.

We have entered a new era in world history

- The kingdom has come near (Matt 4:17; 10:7; Mark 1:15).
- The kingdom has come upon us (Matt 12:28; 2 Tim 4:1).
- The kingdom is among us (Luke 17:20–21).

- The kingdom is being entered (Matt 21:31).

- The kingdom is possessed by God's people (Matt 21:43).

- Prophets, righteous ones, and kings longed to see what we see and hear what we hear (Matt 13:17; Luke 10:23–24).

- Angels yearn to look into the salvation that has been announced to us (1 Pet 1:10–12).

- We experience what that the Scriptures had foretold (Acts 2:14–21; 2:29–36).

- Now is the acceptable time (2 Cor 6:2).

- Now is the day of salvation (2 Cor 6:2).

- The mystery of the ages has been revealed (Col 1:26).

- The end of the ages has come (1 Pet 1:20).

- The fullness of time has come (Gal 4:4–5).

- We have entered into God's Sabbath rest (Heb 4:3, 10–11).

- People are scrambling to get in on our experience of God's kingdom (Luke 16:16–17).

- The pivotal time in world history is here and the masses don't realize it (Luke 12:54–56).

We have entered into a new world reality

- This world's desires are passing away (1 John 2:17).

- The present form of this world is passing away (1 Cor 7:29–31).

- Creation is new (2 Cor 5:17).

- Everything old is passing away (2 Cor 5:17).

- Everything has become new (2 Cor 5:17).

- New creation is everything (Gal 6:15).

- The true light is already shining (1 John 2:8).

- The darkness is passing (1 John 2:8).

- All things in heaven and earth have been reconciled to God through Christ and are at peace (2 Cor 5:18–19; Col 1:20).

- We are the firstfruits of God's creatures (Jas 1:18).

We have entered into a new life

- We are dead to sin (Rom 6:11; Eph 2:1–6).
- We have passed from death to life (John 5:24; 1 John 3:14).
- We have been raised with Christ to life from above (Col 2:12; 3:1).
- We have eternal life (John 3:15, 16, 36; 4:14; 5:24; 6:40, 47; 10:28; 1 Tim 6:12, 19; 1 John 5:11–12).
- We walk in newness of life (Rom 6:4).
- We have been given abundant life (John 10:10).
- We are alive to God (Rom 6:11).
- We are alive together with Christ (Eph 2:5; Col 2:13; 3:3).
- We live forever (1 John 2:8).
- We have living water (John 4:10).
- We have been born from above (Jas 1:18).
- We have been born of God (1 John 3:6, 9; 5:18).
- We have been born anew by the word of God (1 Pet 1:23).
- We have been born again into a living hope (1 Pet 1:3).

We have entered into a new social reality and set of relationships

- We have been reconciled to God through Christ (2 Cor 5:18).
- We no longer view anyone from a human point of view (2 Cor 5:16).
- We are at peace with those from whom we were once estranged (Eph 2:1–17).
- There is no longer Jew or Greek (Gal 3:28; Eph 2:11–15; Col 3:11).
- There is no longer circumcised or uncircumcised (Col 3:11).
- There is no longer slave or free (Gal 3:28; Col 3:11; Phlm 1:16–17).
- There is no longer male or female (Gal 3:28; Acts 2:18).
- There is no longer barbarian or Scythian (Col 3:11).

- We have fellowship with one another (1 John 1:7).

- We have become companions of the Holy Spirit (Heb 6:4).

- We are God's household (1 Pet 4:17).

- We are the new humanity (Eph 1:13–15).

- We have been built together into a dwelling place for God (Eph 2:21–22).

We have entered into a new way of living

- We have come to fullness in Christ (Col 2:10).

- We have been made clean (John 15:3).

- We have been cleansed of sin (1 John 1:7).

- We have been stripped of our old self and clothed with a new self (Col 3:9–10).

- We are clothed in Christ (Gal 3:27).

- We are being renewed according to the image of God (Col 3:10–11).

- We have been washed (Titus 3:5).

- We have been regenerated (Titus 3:5).

- We are children of light (1 Thess 5:4–5).

- We walk in the light (1 John 1:7).

- Truth abides in us and will do so forever (2 John 1:2).

- Our inner nature is being renewed day by day (2 Cor 4:16).

We have entered into a new status

- The least person in God's kingdom is greater than all pre-kingdom people (Luke 7:28).

- God's love reaches perfection in us (1 John 2:5; 4:12, 16, 17).

- The lowly are raised and the rich are being lowered (Jas 1:9–10).

- Our citizenship is in heaven (Phil 3:20).

- The immeasurable greatness of God's power belongs to us (Eph 1:19).

- All things are ours (1 Cor 3:21–23).

- We possess everything (2 Cor 6:10).

- We have been saved (Luke 19:9; Eph 2:5, 8).

- We are being glorified by God (Rom 8:19, 21).

- We are the children of God (Gal 4:4–5; 1 John 3:1–2; 5:19).

- We are Abraham's offspring and heirs to God's promise (Gal 3:29).

- We abide in Jesus (1 John 2:6).

- We are raised up and seated with Christ in heavenly places (Eph 2:6).

- We are God's temple and he lives and walks among us (2 Cor 6:16).

- We are saints or holy ones (Phil 1:10).

- We have become the righteousness of God (2 Cor 5:21).

- We are the aroma of Christ, a fragrance from life to life (2 Cor 2:15–16).

We have entered into God's abundant blessings

- We receive in this life hundredfold houses, family, and fields (Mark 10:29–30; Luke 18:28–30).

- Good news is proclaimed to the poor, captive, and oppressed (Luke 4:18–21).

- The truth has set us free (John 8:32).

- The son has set us free (John 8:36).

- We are free from law, sin, death, and bondage (Rom 8:1–2, 21).

- We are free from this present evil age (Gal 1:4).

- We are free from the elemental spirits of the universe (Col 2:20).

- We have received God's long-awaited Holy Spirit (John 14:16; Acts 2:14–21; 2 Cor 1:22; Eph 1:13; 1 John 3:24; 4:13).

- We have been enlightened (Heb 6:4).

- We have tasted the heavenly gift (Heb 6:4).

- We have tasted God's word (Heb 6:5).

- We have tasted the powers of the coming age (Heb 6:5).

- We have tasted God's goodness (1 Pet 2:2–3).

- We are receiving the salvation of our souls (1 Pet 1:9).

- We are receiving an unshakeable/eternal kingdom (Heb 12:28; 2 Pet 1:11).

What great news! It seems too good to be true. God has not forsaken his creation; he has intervened decisively to create a better place. This means new life in a new reality in world history. It is a new way of relating to people and breaking free from sin. We've been given a new status and showered with abundant blessings.

Accepting the Better Place of Christ's Body

For some, this is hard to accept. It seems so utopian, so detached from everyday life. We find it easier to embrace the idea that new life will be available in some distant time and place. Yet God's better world is exactly what we accept when we enter into Christ. We cannot accept forgiveness of sins and an eternal *after*life without embracing the abundant life and new world that God has called us into *even now* in the body of Christ.

Still, part of us doesn't want this new life to have already begun. We are nervous about it taking shape in and through the ordinary flawed people we find in the church. We don't want God's treasure contained in clay jars (2 Cor 4:7). But that is what God has made of us—and for good reason.

The new and abundant life to which God has called us is God's chosen means of drawing all people to himself. As the firstfruits, we are God's evidence of the fuller crop to come. We don't do God any favors by humbly abstaining from abundant life in the here and now. God is not impressed by our patience and willingness to bide our time while we wait for the afterlife.

God wants us to embrace his gift *now* so we can display and proclaim it to others. What makes firstfruits so hopeful is that they are a promise, a reassurance of more to come. But firstfruits can't act like firstfruits when they don't really believe they are. Though God has more in store for all creation, for the world's sake we must fully embrace what he has already begun among us.

11

God Calls the Church to Display a Better Place

GOD HAS SHOWERED ABUNDANT blessings upon his people. He made us heirs of all things and gave us his Spirit as a deposit (2 Cor 5:5). The Spirit, in turn, has made *us* a sort of deposit. We are the firstfruits of God's saving work in this world (2 Thess 2:13; Jas 1:18). Our role is not only to announce that God intends someday to change this world, but to demonstrate that—in a specific sense—he already has.

Displaying the Kingdom

Jesus constantly talked about the kingdom. It was his core message. He preferred to speak about it in parables. Jesus described it mostly by analogy, saying, "The kingdom of heaven is like . . . ." He didn't walk around saying "Do this" or "Do that." He taught as if the most important message he could impart is what the kingdom *is* and *is not* like. This was his focus even after his resurrection (Acts 1:3). But why?

The answer is quite simple. Jesus intended the kingdom to be the organizing center of the church's life together. The kingdom vision is to the church what Torah was to Israel. Every congregation's life together should look like the kingdom.

When developers plan to build a new subdivision filled with houses of a particular style, it is common for them first to construct a model home in a visible place. They then invite potential buyers to tour this model home. Anyone can walk around in it and get a feel for what life in such a home might be like. This hands-on experience helps them evaluate whether they wish to live in the subdivision to come.

So it is with the church. We are the model home of God's kingdom. To the extent that we display God's kingdom in our life together, God is able to draw people to himself through our witness. Among us they can taste and see the Lord's goodness. We are the evidence that Jesus has changed the course of world history, that he has already begun a new and better world. This new and better world can be experienced now. We are the foretaste of God's perfected world to come.

In this way, the church continues Israel's God-given mission. Starting with Abraham, God formed a people who would become a light to the nations. Jesus gathered these people, reconciled them to God, empowered them by his Spirit, added Gentiles to their number, and sent them into all nations. Their mission is to be and do in every land what Israel began to be and do in Palestine. This was God's plan for his people from the very beginning.

Churches seeking to model the kingdom before the watching world must get a solid grip on what God's kingdom is like. Jesus' parables are a wonderful place to begin, but they are not our only source. In Acts, the Holy Spirit helps Jesus' followers put his teachings into practice as they plant churches throughout the ancient world. In the New Testament letters, prominent leaders guide these same churches through the process of applying Jesus' kingdom vision to various challenges they face.

From the rich witness of the New Testament, we get a pretty good idea what God's kingdom is like:

- It takes precedence over all other loyalties (Matt 6:33; 13:44–46).
- It lives by God's wisdom (1 Cor 1:17–2:16; Jas 3:13–18).
- It produces Christlike citizens (Rom 8:29; 1 Pet 2:21; 1 John 4:17).
- It flees from and repents of immorality (1 Cor 6:18–20; Gal 5:16–21).
- It follows the Holy Spirit's leading (John 16:13–15; Rom 8:13–14).
- It grows in ways only understood by God (Mark 4:26–29; Col 2:18–19).
- It shows equality regardless of gender, race, age, heritage, or social status (2 Cor 5:16–17; Gal 3:26–29; Col 3:9–11).
- It loves God's people sincerely (John 13:34–35; 1 Pet 1:22; 2:17; 4:8).
- It unifies through diversity (John 17:20–24; 1 Cor 12:12–27).
- It forgives and reconciles at all levels (Matt 18:15–35; 2 Cor 5:18–19).

- It seeks peace in all circumstances (Matt 5:38–48; Rom 12:17–21; 1 Pet 3:9–17).

- It values children and childlikeness (Matt 18:1–5; Luke 18:15–17).

- It assumes a humble servant posture (Mark 9:33–35; John 13:1–17).

- It esteems small, unimpressive beginnings (Matt 13:31–32; 1 Cor 1:26–31).

- It welcomes the undeserving and unexpected (Matt 20:1–16; 21:28–32; 22:2–14).

- It draws people in from the margins (Luke 4:18–21; Jas 1:27).

- It assimilates the poor more easily than the wealthy (Matt 19:23–24; Jas 2:5).

- It provides generously for all needs (Acts 4:32–35; 2 Cor 9:7–8).

- It infiltrates the world (Matt 5:13–16; Luke 13:20–21).

- It confuses those who lack God's Spirit (Mark 4:11–20; 1 Cor 2:6–16).

- It attracts frauds as well as genuine converts (Matt 13:24–30; 1 Cor 11:19).

- It rejoices in suffering (Rom 5:3–5; Jas 1:2–4; 1 Pet 4:12–16).

- It raises people to eternal life (John 6:40; 1 Cor 15:12–23).

- It entails a restoration of this earth (Rom 8:18–25; Rev 21).

- It overcomes all powers that oppose it (1 Cor 15:24–28; Col 2:15).

Jesus' kingdom vision functions like a rudder for the church. It determines our direction and guides all that we say and do. It provides the criteria for all the decisions we make. At least, it should. New Testament authors don't use "kingdom" language at every turn to explain what they do and why. They simply implore God's people to order their life together in ways that are worthy of their calling, consistent with the gospel, and befitting those who are in Christ (Eph 4:1; Phil 1:27; Gal 3:28).

The New Testament's Emphasis

The exact language New Testament authors use is less important than their shared emphases. Each author focuses on Jesus as Savior and King; and each one instructs believers to order their life together according to him. Central to this life together is how God's people treat one another. Paul, John, Peter, and others routinely encourage churches to love one another, take care of one another, forgive one another, be unified with one another, and serve one another.

By way of contrast, these authors say very little about how believers ought to treat unbelievers. They clearly expect believers to proclaim the gospel to all people, but they also insist that we remain separate from unbelievers and respectful of worldly powers. Scripture is strikingly silent as to how God's people ought to help out needy unbelievers, improve living conditions for all people in our towns and cities, and speak prophetically to unbelieving institutions that are abusing their power on loan from God.

Though Jesus reminded Pilate that his power came from God, he never gave him tips about how to rule better. Though Paul invoked Roman citizenship to escape illegal and harsh treatment, he never used his status to influence Roman culture or government. He only used it to serve his mission of proclaiming the gospel and strengthening believers in Rome. This stance seems consistent with what Paul taught the Thessalonians:

> Now concerning love of the brothers and sisters, you do not need to have anyone write to you, for you yourselves have been taught by God to love one another; and indeed you do love all the brothers and sisters throughout Macedonia. But we urge you, beloved, to do so more and more, to aspire to live quietly, to mind your own affairs, and to work with your hands, as we directed you, so that you may behave properly toward outsiders and be dependent on no one (1 Thess 4:9–12).

When it came to fellow believers, love was the rule. When it came to outsiders, independence and propriety prevailed. The early church did not feel responsible for the condition and direction of wider society. But they felt deeply responsible for one another and for fellow believers throughout the world.

The "gifts" passages in the New Testament continue this trend. We read in several places that God has gifted every believer by his Spirit. He has granted each one a specific spiritual ability or function. Some are empowered to teach. Others can prophesy, give, help, speak different languages, and so forth. The purpose behind these various gifts is illuminating.

When Jesus bestows gifts upon his people in Ephesians 4, they serve to build up the body until it reaches the fullness of Christ. When the Spirit gives gifts in 1 Corinthians 12–14, they serve to edify the body of Christ. The gifts passage in Romans 12 is no different. It is immediately followed by instruction to "meet the needs of the saints." If meeting the needs of the wider world were an integral part of the Christian calling, the complete absence of any instruction or empowerment for this task is striking. The only gift that seems tailored to serve the wider world is evangelism.

What about Love?

One of the best kept secrets among Bible scholars today is how the New Testament depicts Christian love. New Testament scholar Gerhard Lohfink puts it this way: "In view of contemporary Christian consciousness it comes as something of a shock to realize as an exegete that in the New Testament—if we abstract from Jesus' saying about love of enemy—interpersonal love almost without exception means *love for one's brother in the faith, love of Christians for one another.* There seems to be hardly anything else about the New Testament which is as intensively suppressed as this fact" [original emphasis].[1]

This statement is strong, but true. Scripture teaches us to love fellow believers—not all humans in general. The evidence is so clear and overwhelming that it is hard to believe it is not common knowledge. At the risk of overkill, I quote here from nearly every New Testament passage that instructs believers to love people. I take this risk because we need a wide sampling of Scripture to grasp how much it emphasizes love *for one another* and *not* for all people everywhere. A wider reading is also necessary to overcome selective interpretations that are based on taking one or two passages out of context.

> I give you a new commandment, that you love *one another.* Just as I have loved you, you also should love *one another.* By this everyone will know that you are my disciples, if you have love *for one another.* (John 13:34–35)

---

1. Lohfink, *Jesus and Community,* 110.

This is my commandment, that you love *one another* as I have loved you. No one has greater love than this, to lay down one's life *for one's friends*. (John 15:12–13)

I am giving you these commands so that you may love *one another*. If the world hates you, be aware that it hated me before it hated you. If you belonged to the world, the world would love you as its own. Because you do not belong to the world, but I have chosen you out of the world—therefore the world hates you. (John 15:17–19)

Let love be genuine; hate what is evil, hold fast to what is good; love *one another* with mutual affection; outdo one another in showing honor. (Rom 12:9–10)

Owe no one anything, except to love *one another*; for the one who loves another has fulfilled the law. The commandments, "You shall not commit adultery; You shall not murder; You shall not steal; You shall not covet"; and any other commandment, are summed up in this word, "Love your neighbor as yourself." Love does no wrong to a neighbor; therefore, love is the fulfilling of the law. (Rom 13:8–10)

If *your brother or sister* is being injured by what you eat, you are no longer walking in love. (Rom 14:15)

For you were called to freedom, brothers and sisters; only do not use your freedom as an opportunity for self-indulgence, but through love become slaves *to one another*. For the whole law is summed up in a single commandment, "You shall love your neighbor as yourself." If, however, you bite and devour one another, take care that you are not consumed by one another. (Gal 5:13–15)

I have heard of your faith in the Lord Jesus and your love *toward all the saints*. (Eph 1:15)

I therefore, the prisoner in the Lord, beg you to lead a life worthy of the calling to which you have been called, with all humility and gentleness, with patience, bearing *with one another* in love, making every effort to maintain the unity of the Spirit in the bond of peace. (Eph 4:1–3)

But speaking the truth in love, we must grow up in every way into him who is the head, into Christ, from whom *the whole body*, joined and knit together by every ligament with which it is equipped, as each part is working properly, promotes *the body's* growth in building *itself* up in love. (Eph 4:15–16)

If then there is any encouragement in Christ, any consolation from love, any sharing in the Spirit, any compassion and sympathy, make my joy complete: be of the *same mind*, having the *same love*, being *in full accord and of one mind.* (Phil 2:1–2)

For we have heard of your faith in Christ Jesus and of the love that you have *for all the saints.* (Col 1:4)

For I want you to know how much I am struggling for you, and for those in Laodicea, and for all who have not seen me face to face. I want their hearts to be encouraged and *united in love*, so that they may have all the riches of assured understanding and have the knowledge of God's mystery, that is, Christ himself. (Col 2:1–2)

Above all, clothe *yourselves* with love, which binds everything together in perfect harmony. And let the peace of Christ rule in your hearts, to which indeed you were called *in the one body.* And be thankful. (Col 3:14–15)

And may the Lord make you increase and abound in love *for one another* and for all, just as we abound in love for you. (1 Thess 3:12)[2]

Now concerning love of the *brothers and sisters*, you do not need to have anyone write to you, for you yourselves have been taught by God to love *one another*; and indeed you do love *all*

---

2. This passage comes as close as any in the New Testament to encouraging Christians to love *all* people. However, in Greek it does not say "all people." It just says "all." Moreover, there is a close parallel a few paragraphs later that provides clarification. In 4:9–10, Paul exhorts Thessalonian believers to love one another and *all* the brothers and sisters throughout Macedonia. Here "all" clearly has to do with all Macedonian believers—as opposed to just believers in their local church family. More importantly, in the next two verses, Paul goes on to instruct them how to relate properly toward those *outside* the body. With regard to outsiders, he instructs them to live quietly, mind their own affairs, and be dependent on no one (vv. 11–12). This stands in stark contrast to that interdependent nature of Christian love, which we discuss in chapter 17.

the brothers and sisters throughout Macedonia. But we urge you, beloved, to do so more and more, to aspire to live quietly, to mind your own affairs, and to work with your hands, as we directed you, so that you may behave properly toward outsiders and be dependent on no one. (1 Thess 4:9–12)

We must always give thanks to God for you, brothers and sisters, as is right, because your faith is growing abundantly, and the love of every one of you *for one another* is increasing. (2 Thess 1:3)

When I remember you in my prayers, I always thank my God because I hear of your love *for all the saints* and your faith toward the Lord Jesus. (Phlm 1:4–5)

For God is not unjust; he will not overlook your work and the love that you showed for his sake in *serving the saints,* as you still do. (Heb 6:10)

And let us consider how to provoke *one another* to love and good deeds, not neglecting to meet together, as is the habit of some, but encouraging *one another,* and all the more as you see the Day approaching. (Heb 10:24–25)

Let *mutual* love continue. (Heb 13:1)

Now that you have purified your souls by your obedience to the truth so that you have genuine *mutual* love, love *one another* deeply from the heart. (1 Pet 1:22)

Honor everyone. Love *the family of believers.* Fear God. Honor the emperor. (1 Pet 2:17)

Finally, all of you, have unity of spirit, sympathy, love *for one another,* a tender heart, and a humble mind. (1 Pet 3:8)

Above all, maintain constant love *for one another,* for love covers a multitude of sins. (1 Pet 4:8)

The children of God and the children of the devil are revealed in this way: all who do not do what is right are not from God, nor are those who do not love *their brothers and sisters.* For this is the message you have heard from the beginning, that we should love *one another*. We must not be like Cain who was from the evil one and murdered his brother. And why did he murder him? Because his own deeds were evil and his brother's righteous. Do not be astonished, brothers and sisters, that the world hates you. We know that we have passed from death to life because we love *one another*. Whoever does not love abides in death. All who hate *a brother or sister* are murderers, and you know that murderers do not have eternal life abiding in them. We know love by this, that he laid down his life for us—and we ought to lay down our lives *for one another*. How does God's love abide in anyone who has the world's goods and sees *a brother or sister* in need and yet refuses help? Little children, let us love, not in word or speech, but in truth and action. (1 John 3:10–18)

And this is his commandment, that we should believe in the name of his Son Jesus Christ and love *one another*, just as he has commanded us. (1 John 3:23)

Beloved, let us love *one another*, because love is from God; everyone who loves is born of God and knows God. Whoever does not love does not know God, for God is love. God's love was revealed among us in this way: God sent his only Son into the world so that we might live through him. In this is love, not that we loved God but that he loved us and sent his Son to be the atoning sacrifice for our sins. Beloved, since God loved us so much, we also ought to love *one another*. No one has ever seen God; if we love *one another*, God lives in us, and his love is perfected in us. (1 John 4:7–12)

Love has been perfected *among us* in this: that we may have boldness on the day of judgment, because as he is, so are we in this world. There is no fear in love, but perfect love casts out fear; for fear has to do with punishment, and whoever fears has not reached perfection in love. We love because he first loved us. Those who say, "I love God," and hate their *brothers or sisters*, are liars; for those who do not love *a brother or sister* whom they have seen, cannot love God whom they have not seen. The commandment we have from him is this: those who love God must love their *brothers and sisters* also. (1 John 4:17–21)

> But now, dear lady, I ask you, not as though I were writing you a
> new commandment, but one we have had from the beginning,
> let us love *one another*. (2 John 1:5)

Possible Exceptions

The italicized phrases say it all. The clear teaching of the New Testament
is that Christians ought to love *one another*. Still, Jesus' teachings about
love of neighbor and love of enemy might be understood as exceptions to
this rule. We often assume that neighbor love means universal love for all
people or perhaps love for our next-door neighbors who may or may not
be believers. But in the Old Testament passage Jesus quotes, the neighbor
in question is a fellow Israelite: "You shall not hate in your heart *anyone
of your kin*; you shall reprove your neighbor, or you will incur guilt yourself. You shall not take vengeance or bear a grudge against any of *your
people*, but you shall love your neighbor as yourself: I am the LORD" (Lev
19:17–18). Since Jesus ministered almost exclusively among the Jews, his
teaching about neighbor love conveyed this primary meaning.

But didn't Jesus expand this definition of neighbor to include all
people? Isn't that what the parable of the Good Samaritan is all about?
Not as much as it may seem. Samaritans were Jews too, even though they
were treated as lower-level Jews because they had intermarried with for-
eigners. Jesus was inviting his disciples to reach out to estranged Israelites
whom they considered half-Jews. Remember—God's mission to the Gentiles doesn't begin until Acts 10, and Jesus states elsewhere that he was
only sent to the lost sheep of Israel (Matt 15:24). Samaritan sheep were
simply more lost than others. Jesus treated them in much the same way
he treated Jewish tax collectors and women of disrepute.

Jesus' teaching about enemy love, however, seems to push beyond a
strictly in-house application:

> You have heard that it was said, "You shall love your neighbor
> and hate your enemy." But I say to you, Love your enemies and
> pray for those who persecute you, so that you may be children of
> your Father in heaven; for he makes his sun rise on the evil and
> on the good, and sends rain on the righteous and on the unrigh-
> teous. For if you love those who love you, what reward do you
> have? Do not even the tax collectors do the same? And if you
> greet only your brothers and sisters, what more are you doing

than others? Do not even the Gentiles do the same? Be perfect,
therefore, as your heavenly Father is perfect. (Matt 5:43–48)

This passage could be saying that disciples ought to love fellow disciples
who stand in opposition to them. Gentiles only love fellow Gentiles who
act favorably to them. But God's people are different. We love one another
even when our own people irk us, frustrate us, and cause us grief.

Still, these verses follow on the heels of Jesus' teaching about soldiers forcing Jews to carry their burden across town and other people
slapping them in the face (Matt 5:38–42). These do not seem like strictly
in-house Jewish issues. Even so, the love expressed in these scenarios was
not about entering into an extended relationship of mutual affection and
prioritization as is typical of Christian love.

Many scholars interpret Jesus' unpredictable responses to abuse as
tactics for jolting an oppressor's conscience so they would stop using,
abusing, and publicly humiliating God's people. This is how Paul applies
it in Romans 12:20–21: "If your enemies are hungry, feed them; if they
are thirsty, give them something to drink; for by doing this you will heap
burning coals on their heads. Do not be overcome by evil, but overcome
evil with good."

Neither Jesus nor Paul instructs believers to love their enemies (or
all people in general) in some abstract or systematic way. Rather, they
teach us how to love the specific enemy currently exploiting us. Notice
the kinds of unplanned encounters Jesus brings up when speaking about
enemy love: if anyone strikes you on the cheek, if anyone takes your coat,
if anyone forces you to walk a mile with them. These are concrete flesh
and blood encounters. They are specific instances when people enter our
turf or cross our path in hostile ways. Jesus calls believers to face such
unplanned confrontations with an intentional enemy love posture.

Contemporary parallels would be intruders who break into our
house in order to harm us, steal our possessions, or vandalize our property, or, perhaps, a stranger who unexpectedly assaults us on the street.
Interestingly, many Christians today feel justified to retaliate violently
when faced with these sorts of scenarios. Some will proudly purchase
weapons so they can defend themselves in such instances. But those same
people will often deduce from this passage a universal love for all people
and then claim such love as the biblical basis for making the world a
better place. The plain meaning of the text is abandoned, and a feel-good
teaching that is alien to the text supplants it.

In his teaching on enemy love, Jesus builds on the instruction of Torah. Exodus 23:4–5 reads, "When you come upon your enemy's ox or donkey going astray, you shall bring it back. When you see the donkey of one who hates you lying under its burden and you would hold back from setting it free, you must help to set it free."

In this Old Testament context, an act of kindness to one's enemy exemplifies neighborliness and perhaps serves to reconcile a broken relationship. For Christians today, the face-to-face enemy may not be a believer. Since unbelievers often live next door, we may help bring their dog home after it snaps its chain and wanders about on our property. Our motive would be similar: to lend assistance and perhaps strengthen our relationship, which might ultimately lead them to faith. Even so, living at peace with one's enemies cannot be equated with the kind of love the New Testament expects believers to show one another.

In sum, Jesus' teaching about neighbor love dovetails nicely with what we learn about love throughout the rest of the New Testament. Moreover, his teaching about enemy love provides a path for overcoming enmity between us and specific people who would do us harm, whether believer or unbeliever.

Regardless of how one interprets Matthew 5, the string of "love one another" verses quoted above demonstrates that Jesus' followers took his teaching on love to mean, first and foremost, that believers should love one another. When New Testament authors talk about how we care for unbelievers—beyond witnessing to them—they prefer language of acting nobly (Rom 12:17), extending goodness (Rom 12:21; Gal 6:10; 1 Thess 5:15), acting wisely (Col 4:5–6), living quietly (1 Thess 4:11), behaving properly (1 Thess 4:12), being gentle and courteous (Titus 3:2), and showing honor (1 Pet 2:12, 17). Language of love is strikingly absent.

Beyond Love

This same pattern emerges when we study New Testament teachings on caring for the poor, widow, orphan, and stranger.[3]

---

3. When read in context and in the original language, it appears likely that the hospitality to strangers spoken about in the New Testament most often refers to traveling believers (Matt 25:31–46; Rom 12:13; 1 Tim 5:10; Heb 13:2).

The Least of These

The passage most often quoted to legitimate social activism actually supports what I have been saying. In the parable of the Sheep and Goats, the king—who represents Jesus—welcomes into his kingdom only those who fed him when he was hungry, gave him a drink when he was thirsty, welcomed him when he was a stranger, clothed him when he was naked, cared for him when he was sick, and visited him when he was in prison. Those who were rewarded don't recall doing this for him. So the king reminds them. saying, "just as you did it to one of the least of these *who are members of my family*, you did it to me" (Matt 25:40).

It is common for people to refer to "the least of these" as any needy person in the world, as if Jesus issued a call for global philanthropy. But this reading cuts Jesus' words short. Note the italicized phrase above. It clarifies that Jesus was speaking about his faith family and anticipating the future needs of his disciples. When Jesus said this, his followers were about to scatter throughout the world to proclaim the gospel and plant churches. When they leave behind the security of their homes, they will have to rely upon the generosity of fellow believers whom they encounter along the way. Those who care for *them* will be richly rewarded by God. Those who don't will be punished. That is Jesus' point. This is not some new interpretation I am forcing upon the text. It is represented in one way or another in every translation of Matthew 25.

Widows and Orphans

James's famous teaching about widows and orphans is also misused to promote a universal mandate for philanthropy. It famously reads, "If any think they are religious, and do not bridle their tongues but deceive their hearts, their religion is worthless. Religion that is pure and undefiled before God, the Father, is this: to care for orphans and widows in their distress, and to keep oneself unstained by the world" (Jas 1:26–27).

The language of this passage is generic enough that we can fill it with a variety of different meanings to serve the agenda of our choosing. Only by reading it in its context do we gain a clearer sense of what James had in mind. The first observation to make about these verses is that they preview the letter's content. Religion that bridles the tongue is discussed in chapter 3, caring for widows and orphans is discussed in chapter 2, and keeping unstained by the world is the focus of chapters 4–5. Chapter 1 is an introductory chapter that raises the various themes of the book.

So the key to understanding what James meant by caring for widows and orphans is to note what the wider book of James says about the poor, especially chapter 2. Its most relevant statements are as follows:

> Let *the believer* who is lowly boast in being raised up, and the rich in being brought low, because the rich will disappear like a flower in the field. (Jas 1:9–10)

> My brothers and sisters, do you with your acts of favoritism really believe in our glorious Lord Jesus Christ? For if a person with gold rings and in fine clothes comes *into your assembly*, and if a poor person in dirty clothes also comes in, and if you take notice of the one wearing the fine clothes and say, "Have a seat here, please," while to the one who is poor you say, "Stand there," or, "Sit at my feet," have you not made distinctions *among yourselves*, and become judges with evil thoughts? Listen, my beloved brothers and sisters. Has not God chosen the poor in the world *to be rich in faith and to be heirs of the kingdom* that he has promised to those who love him? But you have dishonored the poor. Is it not the rich who oppress you? Is it not they who drag you into court? Is it not they who blaspheme the excellent name that was invoked over you? You do well if you really fulfill the royal law according to the scripture, "You shall love your neighbor as yourself." But if you show partiality, you commit sin and are convicted by the law as transgressors. (Jas 2:1–9)

> What good is it, my brothers and sisters, if you say you have faith but do not have works? Can faith save you? If a *brother or sister* is naked and lacks daily food, and one of you says to them, "Go in peace; keep warm and eat your fill," and yet you do not supply their bodily needs, what is the good of that? So faith by itself, if it has no works, is dead (Jas 2:14–17).

The problem James confronts is clear. Some upwardly mobile believers were trying to advance their status in the world by showing favoritism to wealthy people in their assemblies. These wealthy persons could be guests, but they may also be regular attendees since James accuses them in verses 1–4 of showing favoritism and making distinctions "among themselves." That is not acceptable because, as he reminds them in 1:9, the *believer* who is lowly is being raised up. This parallels the poor of this world who are *rich in faith* and receive the kingdom (2:5). If believers insist on picking sides, they need to recognize who is truly great in God's kingdom. For James, that means siding with poor believers with great faith.

Having set their world view right side up—by flipping it upside down—James then shows his readers what it looks like in practice. To live by faith is to provide clothing and daily food for brothers and sisters in need. These are the widows and orphans James speaks of in 1:27. There are no other candidates in the book of James. Nor are believers instructed elsewhere in the New Testament to care for widows and orphans outside the family of faith. Orphans aren't even mentioned elsewhere in the New Testament. The widows they care for and are instructed to provide for are fellow believers (Acts 6; 1 Tim 5). The Old Testament testimony is no different (Deut 26:12–13; Isa 10:1–2).[4]

The Poor and Oppressed

Those who persistently remind the church of God's preferential option for the poor and his prevailing tendency to side with the oppressed are not wrong. These themes are certainly present throughout Scripture. We are only wrong when we equate the poor and oppressed of the Bible story with all poor and oppressed people in all times and places. One cannot extract the language of Scripture from the biblical narrative and insert it into any context one wishes.

The Exodus story, for instance, is not the story of God liberating all slaves everywhere from any nation that would enslave them. It is about God liberating Abraham's descendants from Egypt so they may become his servants and live by Torah. When they forsake that commitment, God no longer protects their widows and orphans (Isa 9:13–17). The lowly and hungry of Mary's Magnificat are also the downtrodden people of

---

4. A noteworthy exception, one that Jesus highlights, is the widow of Zarephath, in Sidon (a prosperous coastal town northeast of Israel). Ironically, God appoints her to provide food for Elijah during a great famine that God brought on Israel due to the wickedness of King Ahab. Elijah has to provide for her and her son by way of miracle (Luke 4:24–26; 1 Kgs 17:9–24). This exceptional passage does not overturn the prevailing testimony of Torah and the prophets that God's people must care for widows and orphans among their own people (e.g., Deut 26:12–13; Isa 10:1–2). Though this incident anticipates the future success of including Gentiles of faith into God's people, neither Jesus nor the Old Testament historian uses it to advocate universal philanthropy.

Israel who are awaiting the fulfillment of God's promise to Abraham's descendants (Luke 1:46–55).

Ashamed of the Gospel

The disturbing bottom line is that, in the New Testament, love and service are reserved especially for fellow believers. This is, frankly, embarrassing. It's not what I want my Bible to say. If God cares so much about this world, why doesn't he give his people an important role in fixing it? Why teach us how to live properly in this world if God doesn't want us to infiltrate its structures and wield our superior knowledge to get them on the right track? Why not help all people everywhere? Isn't it selfish to dedicate our time, energy, and resources primarily to the church family?

But here's the thing: If God is who we say he is—if he is the almighty creator whose knowledge and love for this world is infinite—then he knows better than us what is best for this world. If his wisdom seems foolish to us, it is because we have failed to grasp the genius of his perfect plan. It is because we are still thinking like the world and not paying close attention to God's Word and God's Spirit.

It makes sense to think that focusing our love on fellow believers is excessively insular. But that is not God's logic. If we continue to think that way, then we have missed the strategy behind God's mission. He has called us to embrace and display his reign because that is how he plans to draw *all people* to himself. Our life together is, in God's view, the most powerful force he is willing to exert in order to woo all people to himself. Jesus says it most memorably, "By this everyone will know that you are my disciples, if you have love for one another" (John 13:35).

Jesus' prayer a few chapters later shows just how persuasive Christian unity in love can be: "The glory that you have given me I have given them, so that they may be one, as we are one, I in them and you in me, that they may become completely one, *so that the world may know* that you have sent me and have loved them even as you have loved me" (John 17:22–23).

Our loving unity is how God wishes to convince the world that God sent Jesus. It is God's way of convincing unbelievers that he has intervened in history for the whole world's sake. Jesus has not glorified us so we can bask in that glory, but so we can reflect his glory to others. He has glorified us so we can be savory salt, bright light, and shining stars—a community that displays his kingdom and his righteousness in every aspect of its life together.

Since loving one another is God's plan, it must become our highest priority. No more embarrassment. No more second guessing. No more imitating worldly strategies for making this world a better place. They have failed and will continue to fail. The old order is passing. Only God's kingdom will stand. New creation is everything!

Nothing is more arrogant and self-serving than assuming that we know better than God what is best for *his* world. If God's strategy requires a people whose life together reflects his kingdom, then any other strategy is apostasy and any doctrine that competes with it is heresy.

But how will the world come to know this community that embraces God's reign? How will it encounter their wonderful display of God's kingdom?

We must boldly proclaim it!

12

God Calls the Church to Proclaim a Better Place

"PREACH THE GOSPEL AT all times. When necessary, use words."

We don't know who said these famous words, though many think it was Saint Francis of Assisi. Not long ago, I visited a website dedicated to Saint Francis and an advertisement popped up saying, "Act now to end world hunger." This association makes sense. Francis is remembered for helping the poor, so it is easy to associate him with such lofty and noble goals. But Francis is the patron saint of animals, not world betterment. He made no attempt to end global poverty and probably would have opposed the idea. To him, poverty was true freedom. He strove to liberate people from their possessions.

It is beyond dispute, however, that Saint Francis helped the poor. He did so quite often. Yet we should not ignore the context of his life and then project modern agendas into it. Francis lived in the twelfth century, the age of the crusades, the age of Christendom. To be Italian was to be Christian. To help a neighbor was to help *a brother or sister in Christ*. Francis was a dedicated churchman. In a vision, Christ called him to repair the church—not the world.

Not Impressed

Francis was also a fiery preacher. He made frequent use of words. They meant a lot to him, and they mean a lot in the New Testament witness. In our day, it is common to hide behind deeds. We assume that if we meet enough needs, feed enough bellies, and help enough children then people will beat down the church's doors to get in. Yet the sad truth is that our good deeds rarely have this effect. Sure, they are received gratefully. Every once in a while a church will even gain positive press coverage for public acts of philanthropy.

But let's face it, we're not the only ones helping people, and the help we offer seldom impresses. When viewed alongside the philanthropy of rich entrepreneurs, our efforts to make this world better seem rather unremarkable. Take, for example, the Giving Pledge. In June 2010, Bill Gates and Warren Buffet teamed up to recruit the wealthiest people of this world—billionaires in particular—to give the majority of their net worth to charitable causes.[1] Within three months, forty individuals pledged $125 billion.[2] Since then, over a hundred individuals or couples have joined them. In 2014, Facebook founder Mark Zuckerberg donated twenty-five million dollars to help fight the Ebola virus. A year later, to celebrate the birth of their daughter, he and his wife publicly committed 99 percent of their Facebook shares to the mission of making this world a better place.[3] At that time, this amounted to forty-five billion dollars.

It may be that, over the centuries, the church has collectively out-given the world. In terms of sweat equity, I am sure this is the case. But that matters little when it comes to public perception of the church. In the minds of unbelievers, we do not stand out in our generosity to needy causes. Politicians, athletes, actors, and wealthy philanthropists seem just as concerned and far more efficient.

We do stand out, in the minds of many, for our religious propaganda.[4] Rather than join the wider circle of humanitarians who are committed to helping people with no strings attached, many Christians feel obligated to share Jesus with people and put Bibles in their hands. When we proclaim our faith while giving out bread, we get seriously reprimanded. Sometimes the church's work is even demonized and compared to the crusades or other forms of imperialistic evangelism. These are, indeed, shameful parts of our legacy and they continue to bear rotten fruit.

As a result, when churches show up to offer disaster relief, we are seldom permitted on the front lines. More often than not, we are sent to

1. For more information, visit http://www.givingpledge.org/.

2. Blackburn, "The Giving Pledge."

3. Full text of their commitment is available at https://www.facebook.com/notes/mark-zuckerberg/a-letter-to-our-daughter/10153375081581634/.

4. See, for example, http://www.huffingtonpost.com/suhag-a-shukla-esq/bread-not-bibles-for-nepal-_b_7192146.html.

the back of the line behind countless other humanitarian organizations and eager public servants. It may look good in the church newsletter, but few churches are recognized by outsiders for having made a substantial difference.

But that's not the real problem. We seek to praise God rather than other people, so lack of worldly praise should not cause us to cease our works of charity. Our aim is to bear witness to God's kingdom. The real issue at stake is how the church brings unbelievers into meaningful contact with God's kingdom. Many have assumed that this contact occurs with actions, not words. This assumption risks turning a much needed corrective against cheap talk and coercive evangelism into the right to remain silent. The New Testament teaches otherwise.

Witness to the World

The New Testament speaks of the church's relationship to the world in many different ways. This variety makes it easy for people to pick and choose passages that speak about this relationship whatever ways they like best. Moralists focus on passages that address the world's need to repent. Separatists focus on passages that emphasize the gap between church and world. Activists focus on passages that call for good works and care for the needy.

Such agenda-driven approaches make it easy to forget the primary way God has called his people to relate to the world. The way forward, again, will be to attend to the broad witness of the New Testament. Below is a concise summary of how various portions of the New Testament call believers to relate to unbelievers:

In the Gospels

- Jesus focuses on proclaiming the kingdom and recruiting followers to do the same (Luke 4:43; 9:60).

- Jesus sets his followers apart as witnesses to all that he said and did (Acts 1:8).

- Jesus calls his followers to fish for people and to make disciples who are like him (Matt 4:19; 28:19–20).

- Jesus anticipates a day when the gospel will be proclaimed to the entire world (Matt 24:14).

- Jesus recognizes that the world will often reject the gospel message and its messengers (Luke 10:11; John 15:18–20).

In Acts

- Jesus sends his followers to be witnesses to the ends of the earth (Acts 1:8).

- The apostles constantly testify to Jesus, the resurrection, and the kingdom (Acts 8:12; 17:15; 28:31).

- The apostles strive to speak the word of God boldly (Acts 4:29).

- Paul summarizes his mission in terms of proclaiming the good news (Acts 20:24–25).

In Paul's Letters

- Paul repeatedly expresses his desire to proclaim the good news to places that have not heard it (Rom 15:19–20).

- Paul reiterates Jesus' commission to proclaim the gospel, whether or not it is convenient (2 Tim 4:1–2).

- Paul underscores the church's responsibility to appeal to the world on God's behalf (2 Cor 5:15–21).

- Paul implores believers to live quietly and wisely among outsiders and to be prepared to speak to them graciously and convincingly as opportunities arise (Col 4:5–6; 1 Thess 4:11–12).

- Paul encourages believers to respect public authorities and not to interfere with their work (1 Tim 2:1–4).

- Paul warns believers against partnering with unbelievers (2 Cor 6:14–18).

The Remaining Letters

- James warns against befriending the world and pursuing worldly agendas (Jas 4:4).

- Peter summarizes the church's purpose in terms of proclaiming God's mighty acts on our behalf (1 Pet 2:9).

- Peter insists that we conduct our lives honorably among the Gentiles so they may see our way of life and come to honor God (1 Pet 2:11–12).

- Peter encourages believers who are subordinate to unbelievers to live in such a way that they may be won over to faith (1 Pet 3:2).

- John speaks of believers as those who have conquered the world and must not be drawn to worldly things (1 John 2:13–16).

- The undeniable heroes of Revelation are those witnesses who hold fast to their testimony to Jesus and to the word of God (Rev 6:9; 12:11; 20:4).

This list isn't comprehensive, but it captures the core essence of how the New Testament teaches believers to relate to unbelievers. All passages presuppose that those who are inside the faith are very different from those who are outside it. Believers and unbelievers are not "basically about the same thing." They have fundamentally different life agendas. Most agendas lead to death; only the path of Christ leads to eternal life.

These passages also make clear that verbal proclamation is central to Christian mission. People will not know what God has accomplished in our lives and for the world unless we tell them. They won't be able to connect the dots simply by observing our good deeds and pious lives. It doesn't matter whether we refer to our proclamation as testimony, witness, disciple-making, or fishing. What matters is that we verbally proclaim the gospel. These terms differ in small ways from one another, but they share a common commitment: each *verbally* introduces unbelievers to God's kingdom and invites them into it.

Not a Priority

It comes as a surprise to many evangelicals that relating to unbelievers is a minor theme in most New Testament books and altogether absent from several of them. More important, by far, is how believers relate to one another. Yet how we relate to one another is directly connected to how we relate to unbelievers. *The primary issue the New Testament addresses is how the Holy Spirit led Jesus and his followers to bring unbelievers into contact with the better place God has created his people to be in this world.* The Gentiles' path to salvation was no different from the path Jesus set before the Jews. They must embrace God's kingdom and join Jesus' followers in displaying it in their life together before the wider world.

Most New Testament churches struggled with the same problem Israel encountered in the Old Testament. They struggled to order their life together according to God's design and mission for them. When the church's life is out of step, it needs to focus on *in-house* proclamation. Its disobedience and disorder indicates that many on the inside have not fully embraced the kingdom. That makes it almost impossible for outsiders to regard the better world that the church proclaims as an attractive offer.

Scripture does not focus more on the life of God's people because believers are more important than unbelievers. Rather, it is precisely because unbelievers are so important to God that he focuses on getting his primary instrument—the people of God—into the shape necessary for reaching unbelievers.

Preaching the gospel at all times is, indeed, the church's calling. But in the New Testament, we are not instructed to do so by finding and fixing the world wherever and whenever it is broken. We do so by embracing God's vision of a better world, displaying that better world in our life together, and proclaiming that better world to all who might enter it.

13

God Makes This World the Very Best Place

Recapping the Bible Story

WE ARE NEARLY FINISHED retelling the Bible's story of a better place. That story began by recognizing that God created this world to be very good. It was pregnant with potential both for human thriving and corruption. Humans abused their responsibility to unfold creation's potential. They overstepped the limits God placed upon them. In doing so, they sullied God's world with sin.

Sin distorted every facet of creaturely existence. Violence and oppression rapidly escalated. All creation soon writhed in pain. God was grieved and stepped in to keep things from completely unraveling. With the flood he stopped the bleeding. Through a series of strategic initiatives, he restrained the havoc one person or city could wreak. He established a system of powers and principalities with the potential to make this fallen world a better place. Even where they fail to accomplish that task, the powers at least keep the world from spinning too far out of control.

All of this sets up God's most strategic initiative, which dominates the rest of the Bible story. Through Abraham and his descendants, God formed a people whose way of life exemplified God's will in our fallen world and paved the way for the better place God ultimately intended to make of this world. Somehow all nations would be blessed through them, though they were not sure exactly how.

The Israelites complicated God's mission for them by turning their backs on his will for their life together. They adopted poor substitutes borrowed from other nations. Yet God remained faithfully by their side and counteracted each act of rebellion with disciplinary correctives.

Having experienced two exiles, God's people grew weary of battling against God and the nations. They longed for a day when God would forgive their transgressions, subdue their enemies, raise their heads, make them a blessing to the nations, and bring all creation into proper alignment with his original intentions.

That day began when God sent Jesus. God's people expected Jesus to defeat their enemies, take control of Palestine, build Israel into a powerful nation, and then use that nation to restore order and advance God's kingdom throughout the world. Eventually, they thought, God would recreate this world as the better place promised through the prophets.

Jesus both exceeded and fell short of these expectations when he inaugurated God's kingdom smack dab in the middle of the old fallen order. First-century Jews imagined the kingdom's coming to be the last step, not the first. They expected Jesus to secure Palestine as the beachhead from which to control the world. Yet Jesus assumed control of the cosmos and promised to secure all lands later. They expected Jesus to restore all creation first and then prosper his people. Yet the renewal and glorification of God's children well precedes the restoration of all other things.

God knew what he was doing. This was his plan all along. In order to give all people an opportunity to embrace his reign, God initiated it first among his people. This allowed them to display God's kingdom and proclaim his invitation for all to enter it. God's people would be God's better place, on display for the world to see. They would experience God's new world long before its completion and they would become expert witnesses of its life-giving abundance. The kingdom would become their new reality. It would position them perfectly to extend God's offer for all people to accept or reject.

Finishing the Bible Story

How will it all end? Since Jesus' first coming was such a surprise, it makes sense to avoid saying too much about his second coming. There is wisdom in this. It often seems in Scripture that God gives his people enough knowledge about the future only to make right decisions in the present.

Yet however surprising his first coming was, Jesus did nothing that was contrary to the content of the prophets' visions. He simply revealed

God's unexpected timing. The New Testament anticipates that the Lord will return and eliminate all powers that oppose him. It expects that God will restore all creation and fulfill Israel's hopes for a better world. The created order still awaits the bodily resurrection of all who died while seeking first God's kingdom.

The renewed world to come—the very best place that God has always intended creation to be—builds upon the new creation that God began in Christ and his new covenant people. Human actions do not slowly progress in reforming or repairing the old fallen order. That order is passing away. Rather, the renewed world to come will complete God's dramatic interruption of world history in creating a new humanity amid the old.

This new humanity—the church—already displays God's love, justice, equality, and economics. How much more will divine righteousness and truth shine brilliantly in the complete renewal to come? The goodness of God's kingdom that the church already experiences and displays in a fragmentary way will become the prevailing reality of all creation. The old order of sin, death, and corruption will no longer exist to hold it back.

Revelation depicts this hope in terms of a New Jerusalem descending from heaven to earth (chs. 21–22). God takes up residence in the new heavens and earth. Enmity and death are gone, for God has eliminated his foes and restored access to the tree of life. All wars have ended, all wounds healed, all tears dried. A river flows from God's throne that sustains all life, and Jesus reigns by God's side.

In the Gospels, Jesus describes the kingdom as a great banquet (Matt 22; Luke 22:30) at which his followers feast alongside Israel's heroes of old (Matt 8:11). Isaiah fills out this picture with images of lions, bears, wolves, and snakes peacefully living alongside lambs, cows, and young children (Isa 11:6–9). *God's very best place neither replaces this world nor reverts back to life before the fall. It is the full flowering of this creation in all of its goodness and potential.*

Only then will God's people uniquely rule over the earth (Matt 19:28; Rev 5:10). This time, they will respect the limits of their dominion, for the throne of God and of the slain lamb will occupy a prominent place in the New Jerusalem (Rev 22:1).

Completing the Better Place Typology

In chapter 2, I introduced three incomplete visions of a better place. I promised to complete this typology by suggesting a better alternative after telling the Bible story. We are now ready to see the whole picture.

BETTER PLACE TYPOLOGY II

	Salvation in Heaven	Salvation on Earth	Restoration began with Jesus	Future interruption	God replaces fallen order	Christians begin fixing fallen order
Heaven Centered	X			X	X	
Human Centered		X				X
World Centered		X	X	X		X
Kingdom Centered		X	X	X	X	

The heaven-centered view emphasizes leaving this world and going to a better place. The human-centered view emphasizes steady human progress as we make this world a better place. The world-centered view invites humans to make this world a better place in anticipation of the better place that God will ultimately make of this world.

We have already explained the weaknesses of each approach. Perhaps the biggest weakness occurs in all of them: each one distorts the role of God's people. We have traced the role of God's people throughout Scripture, and now we can say with relative certainty that God nowhere commissions his people to take the lead in fixing or even maintaining this broken world. We are told instead that this responsibility belongs to governing authorities, who are sometimes called powers and principalities. We are also warned against usurping their authority or otherwise interfering with their work.

The devil unsuccessfully tempted Jesus in the wilderness to do this very thing. The disciples faced the same temptation. When they kept asking Jesus who would be the greatest or who would sit on his right and left in the kingdom, they were asking for authority to govern the world. We often assume that they wanted such power in order to satisfy their lust for control, but that's neither fair to them nor consistent with the New Testament's context. It makes more sense to view them as being misguided about how Jesus' kingdom vision would be implemented.

The disciples wanted the same thing many Christians want today. They wanted to replace bad pagan rulers with good Christian ones. They wanted to make this world a better place in Jesus' name. Jesus knew that their motives were noble, so he didn't reprimand them for harboring evil intent. Rather, he informed them that Gentile authorities also see themselves as benefactors who claim to seek the best interests of all people (Luke 22:25). Yet God has not called his followers to rule this world—not even with good intentions and kingdom principles.

Jesus then reminds them what God's kingdom is like: the greatest becomes like the least, the leader a servant (Luke 22:26–27). That's usually where people stop reading this passage. But the next several verses are crucial: "You are those who have stood by me in my trials; and I confer on you, just as my Father has conferred on me, a kingdom, so that you may eat and drink at my table in my kingdom, and you will sit on thrones judging the twelve tribes of Israel" (vv. 28–30).

Jesus' disciples needed no power over the kingdoms of this world because God had given them a different kingdom with a different view of power. They already occupied important posts in Jesus' kingdom and, in time, they would serve as judges among God's people. Presiding over rival human kingdoms was not their place. That would actually be a demotion!

What role do God's people play now that Jesus has inaugurated God's kingdom and conferred it upon us? Our role is *to be the better place* that God has already made in this world. I call this the "kingdom-centered" view because the role of the church centers on embracing, displaying, and proclaiming God's kingdom. There is no side agenda to make this world a better place—no dual commission.

To truly embrace, display, and proclaim God's kingdom is a full-time, all-encompassing vocation. We cannot serve two masters (Matt 6:24). Loving one another in ways that reflect God's kingdom cannot be accomplished one hour on Sunday and a second hour midweek. The kind of community whose mutual service attracts unbelievers (who don't experience anything like it anywhere else) requires a major reshuffling of schedules, which leaves little room for moonlighting among the power centers of social change.

This view is not kingdom centered because it wants something different than all the other views. It is kingdom centered because, while desiring this world to be the best possible place, it takes God's people to be the firstfruits of such a place. That place is God's kingdom. God wants us to embrace, display, and proclaim this new order rather than partner with the powers to make the old world order that is passing just a little bit better.

The kingdom-centered view presumes a view of social responsibility quite different from other views. We are responsible to do only what God has set us apart to do. We do not assume responsibility for making this world a better place

- even if we have created part of the mess that Western culture is now in,

- even if we gain more wealth and influence than the early church had,

- even if we know more than the powers and have a solid track record of godliness,

- even if we could make a positive difference, and

- even if we suspect that the world will perish unless we do something.

The kingdom-centered view gives up the desire to make this world a better place and embraces instead the church's unique commission of being God's better place in this world. It agrees with the heaven- and world-centered views that God will someday intervene in world history to set the whole world straight. It affirms with the human- and world-centered views that the salvation to come is located on this earth. It agrees with the world-centered view that God has already begun his saving work in human history. But it disagrees with all views that hold Christians responsible for doing whatever they can to fix the fallen order.

It's not that the kingdom-centered view wants the world to get worse. Rather, it is not interested in dressing up the old order in new clothes. God's plan for his people involves embracing, displaying, and proclaiming a new world. This is not for believers' own sake. God's ultimate purpose is that as many unbelievers as possible might encounter and embrace God's kingdom.

If I am right about the role of God's people in Scripture, then the kingdom-centered view most accurately reflects God's vision for the church and world. This will likely make some readers uneasy. Am I saying that Christians shouldn't have any part in organizations that help the needy? Should missionaries ignore social issues and just stick to saving souls? Doesn't that mean that congregations will become insular and disconnected from wider society and its concerns?

No. It doesn't.

What remains now is to put the kingdom-centered view to the test—to discuss its implications where they seem most likely to be misunderstood. This sort of examination comprises the third and final part of this book.

Part Three:

A Better Place in Action

14

The Better Place in Action

THIS WORLD IS TRULY broken *and* God cares deeply about its fallen condition. He has already taken decisive steps toward making it better. Long ago, he began using the powers and principalities to keep violence, lawlessness, and poverty in check. Beginning with Abraham, God formed a set-apart people to show the world the better way he has in mind for his creation.

The earthly ministry of Jesus signaled a decisive turning point in world history. He inaugurated God's better world right in the midst of the fallen one. He made a new humanity of God's set-apart people so they may serve as the firstfruits of God's better world. Their life together participates in the new creation that began with Jesus and anticipates the completion of God's new creation when Jesus returns.

Nonhuman creation must wait for that day before it directly experiences the restoration God has in store. God's people need not wait because God already began this restoration with us. For this reason, God's people bear the meaning and direction of world history. We know what it means and where it is going. We display it in our life together.

Neither ISIS nor the Pentagon knows the way. They certainly don't display it. The powers of this world think that their economy, military, and technology put them in control of world history. They are wrong.

The church bears the direction of world history because it worships the Lord of world history. The church does not pave the way for the world's future; Christ *is* the way and he has already established its future. The church walks in this way and points others to it. Following Israel, we receive God's calling as a gift. But the church has no reason to be proud of its status; it is entirely God's accomplishment at work in us.

To Rule or to Receive

Since it bears the meaning of world history, the church is truly special—more special than we'd like to admit, and more important than we realize. Unfortunately, in the times we *do* realize this, we often take it the wrong way. We want to usurp control of the world's future. We think that our superior knowledge entitles us to positions of power and influence. To be in the know, we assume, is to be in the lead—to be in charge.

This is what the disciples were thinking when they asked Jesus, "Who is the greatest in the kingdom of heaven?" (Matt 18:1). They wanted to know who would be in charge. Who would have the power to influence this world for good? Who would have the authority to make things right?

This is why Jesus responds by saying, "Truly I tell you, unless you change and become like children, you will never enter the kingdom of heaven. Whoever becomes humble like this child is the greatest in the kingdom of heaven" (vv. 3–4).

Jesus wasn't suggesting that the disciples stop being adults by becoming immature and forgetting their experiences. He wasn't praising youthful innocence and playfulness. What Jesus wants from his disciples is a childlike humility.

Though they may not always like it, children accept that they live in a world run by adults. They don't really want that to change. They like that someone else does the work, provides the food, and protects the home. Certainly, they push against the boundaries at times, but they thrive in a world with boundaries that are not theirs to establish.

The longer people live, the less they appreciate boundaries that others have established. They become adult-like and want to change things. The disciples were like that. They didn't mind following Jesus for a time. Every student needs a teacher, they probably thought. They could remain in their place for a while, but eventually things must change. They dreamed of when they would be in charge. And that leads them to quarrel over who is greater. Jesus responds by teaching them about the real nature of things: their job is to serve, not to rule (Luke 22:24–27).

To the world, greatness means power over others. To Jesus, greatness means faithful service in the greatest kingdom. But God's people do not bring that kingdom. We are no different from Israel in that regard. Jesus brought God's kingdom when barely anyone was paying attention. A group of Jews called Zealots were already trying to take the kingdom from Rome by force. A group of Jewish rulers called Sadducees were already trying to gain influence within the Roman establishment by infiltrating its power centers and making tactical alliances.

Jesus came and simply announced it: the kingdom had come. God was doing it. Believe it! Receive it! It's good news for the meek, poor, hungry, and persecuted. It's good news for those who have no power to do anything. Such powerlessness perfectly positions them to humbly receive everything.

When a child receives a new bike for her birthday, she takes to the streets. She sits tall and parades around the block, stopping at all her friends' houses to show off her new bike. "Look what I have!" she exclaims. The child doesn't turn to her parents and say, "Wait a minute! Where'd you get this? How'd you get this? I want to make things like this. I want to manufacture and distribute them as I see fit."

What would a church look like if all its members embraced God's kingdom like children embrace a gift? What would it look like if we stopped striving to make this world into the kingdom and started receiving the kingdom like a gift and displaying it in every aspect of our life together? Wouldn't we be bearing the lighter burden that Jesus spoke about (Matt 11:30), having removed the weight of running or fixing the world from our shoulders?

How would our meek, poor, downtrodden neighbors receive our witness to a better world—a world in which their lowly status does not disqualify or demote them? Would it be good news to them that neither their dead-end jobs nor dysfunctional families need to define them? Who would notice if we were to parade this sort of kingdom around our cities?

Let's imagine we did this. Imagine we proclaimed a kingdom where the least are the greatest. We tell our struggling neighbors the good news. We tell them to taste and see the goodness of God's kingdom. We invite them to church. What do they experience there? Are they greeted joyfully and without discrimination? Or do we size them up like people at work do? Are they welcomed into our homes and around our kitchen tables and fireplaces? Or are they funneled into assimilation programs in commercially carpeted conference rooms? What does our life together say about the kingdom we proclaim?

The Proof is in the Pudding

In this final section, Part Three, I explore several practical areas that are impacted by the church's calling to *be the better place* rather than *make this world a better place*. I frequently attend to the biblical story, paying special attention to what Jesus and the apostles taught about the kingdom. This practice keeps us grounded in the biblical space and yields much fruit. It also helps us test what we've been thinking about. Does my argument mesh with what the New Testament teaches about other topics? Does the framework I'm proposing make better sense of the biblical story than the frameworks I'm arguing against?

For these reasons, I discuss the New Testament's teaching on a variety of topics and show how that teaching naturally fits within the framework proposed in this book. What is more, it will be evident that the New Testament approach to these topics wouldn't make much sense if the responsibility of God's people were heaven- or world-centered. It makes the most sense if we realize that God's people *are* the better place, and that we have been called to a *kingdom*-centered mission.

There are a few things to note as we head into the following chapters. First, I've organized them intentionally. They are not best read by themselves, but in symphony with other chapters, especially those of Part Two. Second, rather than bring these subjects into conversation with all the positions covered in Part One's typology, I revisit the two most popular positions: the heaven-centered and world-centered views. That said, nearly everything I say about the world-centered view applies just as much, if not more, to the human-centered view. Both are committed to making this world a better place. Third, I've clustered the practices I discuss into two groups. The first group has to do with the church's life together: discipleship, leadership, fellowship, family relationships, and friendship. The second focuses directly upon service in and to the wider world: vocation, mission, and witness to the powers.

Entire books can and have been written about each of these topics. So I am neither attempting nor claiming to address them completely and offer some sort of final word on them. Rather, my intention is to show the fundamental coherence between how the New Testament discusses such topics and how that supports the basic thesis of this book. The collective force of these chapters should raise additional questions of application. I address the most common of these questions in the appendix.

15

Discipleship

THE CHURCH PLAYS A big part in the story of God's salvation. Yes, God has saved us and our presence is, indeed, a sign that the world has changed. But we are not simply "saved ones" or even "world changers." We are more than that. We are the new humanity. We are the firstfruits of the new world God has begun. We are pioneers and forerunners who follow the path of Jesus, the pioneer and perfecter of our faith (Heb 12:2).

We don't focus on the church because of the church, but because of God. We trust God and agree with his Word. To do otherwise is to lack faith. Scripture is realistic about the sinfulness and weakness of God's people. From testament to testament, it holds nothing back about our failures and frailties.

Still, God has assigned his people an indispensable place at the center of his plan. God seems to have chosen us precisely *because* we are weak and wayward without him. In him we are strong, and in his strength we boldly proclaim the new creation he has begun with us. It is not humility to act as if this were not so. It is hubris. It presumes that we know better than God.

Membership in Christ's Body

This hubris is at work whenever someone chooses Jesus, but rejects the church. When believers make Christ the center of their lives without participating in a local church, they are trying to act out of their own strength. Jesus is head of the *church*, not the private Lord of pious individuals who want to live right and do good in this world. God's better world is made possible by the work of Christ, and it is made visible in the body of Christ. We cannot seek first God's kingdom without joining the people who embrace, display, and proclaim that kingdom.

A Christian without a church is like a running back without a football team, a shortstop without a baseball team, a setter without a volleyball team. It isn't enough for athletes to self-identify as a running back, a shortstop, or a setter. They must practice and play *with the team*. They must identify with its victories and defeats, its cheers and jeers. They must wear the team insignia, cooperate with their trainers, and adapt their play to the strengths and weakness of the team as a whole.

There is room to disagree with fellow teammates and even denounce poor sportsmanship. For members of the church who have been hurt by other members, this is very important to hear. Nevertheless, to abandon the team on account of displeasure with other players, frustration with team performance, or even because other team members have behaved cruelly, is to leave the coach as well. Professional athletes wouldn't dare quit the team and then call the coach the next day asking for private lessons so they can perform better at family picnics and intermural leagues. Jesus promised to be with the church always (Matt 18:20; 28:18–20). He never vowed to follow individual disciples wherever they might wander.

Authentic disciples truly plug into a local body of Christ. They enter fully into church life, form deep friendships with other members, and build a new life together with them. Attending one or two weekly meetings, giving a set portion of your income, and finding a few concrete ways to serve the body will not do. If the church were a social club or a community service group, that might be enough. But it doesn't reflect the kingdom. It doesn't proclaim the gospel and convey new creation. It's like an athlete who suits up, walks onto the field with the team, but then wanders around the field aimlessly while the game goes on around her.

Not all congregations require true commitment from their members, but that doesn't let disciples off the hook (1 Cor 3:12–15). Church leaders often worry that raising the standard will drive people away. They are right. Jesus had that effect on many people. The strength of our witness depends on the strength of our life together: they will know we are Christians by our love for one another (John 13:35). Church leaders usually don't lower the bar because they want to, but because they fear a loss of numbers. We need to encourage our leaders with eager involvement.

We need to spur one another on to the same level of commitment (Heb 10:24). Our witness is on the line. Our mission hangs in the balance.

The most dangerous religion is not Islam, nor is it atheism (if we want to call that a religion). The most dangerous religion is a form of Christianity that uses the name of Jesus to keep people happy and healthy, but doesn't call them into a form of fellowship that showcases God's kingdom before the watching world.

Moving Beyond Spirituality

> Now there was a Pharisee, a man named Nicodemus who was a member of the Jewish ruling council. He came to Jesus at night and said, "Rabbi, we know that you are a teacher who has come from God. For no one could perform the signs you are doing if God were not with him." Jesus replied, "Very truly I tell you, no one can see the kingdom of God unless they are born again." (John 3:1–3, NIV)

Discipleship means following the Jesus of the whole Bible story. It cannot mean picking and choosing whatever attitudes and actions from his life most agree with us. We can't reduce his life to a generic form of spirituality. Jesus' own life centered on gathering a specific group of people (Abraham's descendants), revealing and entrusting his kingdom to them, and commissioning them to bear witness to his kingdom to the ends of the earth. True disciples don't just imitate Jesus' ethic; they also embrace his mission.

In Jesus' day, there were many Jewish groups who sought to lead God's people into the future they believed God had in store. The Zealots I referred to in the previous chapter sought to gain Jewish national independence by breaking Roman rule over God's people. They used righteous revolutionary violence. From the Roman perspective, they were religious extremists. Today they might be called terrorists. Another group known as the Essenes believed that such resistance was futile. Only God could bring down the powerful Roman Empire. So they migrated away from wider society and formed a Jewish commune in the desert where they could pursue a life of purity and unhindered devotion to God.

The Sadducees rejected both of these approaches. They were the realists. Rome is here to stay, they thought. There is nothing the Jews could do to change that. Their actions followed logically. In order to maintain some semblance of Jewish life, they needed to make peace with

Roman occupation and become friends with foreign rulers. Through tactical alliance and strategic compromise, the Sadducees were able to negotiate certain unique privileges for the Jewish people. For instance, they were allowed to keep and maintain their sacred temple in Jerusalem.

It isn't too hard to see why Jesus didn't join these groups. The kingdom that the Zealots sought was too small, their weapons too weak, and their victories too fleeting. The Essenes stayed too far from the people Jesus sought to save. The Sadducees were too close to the ones Jesus was saving them *from*.

It is more difficult to explain why Jesus didn't pitch his tent with the Pharisees. They wanted what all good people want: to be pure, to live holy lives, and to raise good families. Some of them were hypocritical, as Jesus observed, but their overall agenda was noble. They mingled among the common people and did their best to answer tough questions about how to apply the laws of Moses. This was an important and necessary task because first-century Jews found themselves in a situation that was drastically different from the Israelites who first received God's laws. Jesus didn't think that the Pharisees' teachings were too far off. He taught his followers to obey them (Matt 23:3).

So why didn't Jesus join the Pharisees? Why not banish the hypocrites among them, purify their agenda, and capitalize on their connections and momentum? Why not draw twelve well-trained and articulate disciples from among the Pharisees in order to represent Israel's renewal?

Why? Because Jesus had a different agenda. He wasn't just doing better what the Pharisees were doing. His agenda was fundamentally unlike theirs. The Pharisees launched a people-purifying movement; Jesus initiated a people-mobilizing movement. They purified individuals within old Jewish realities; he created a new social reality. Jesus wasn't content to make individuals right with God; he formed a community that was united in him and mobilized for the kingdom.

Right living never made anyone a disciple of Jesus. As Nicodemus learned in the quote above, disciples needed to be born again. They needed to leave behind their old ways of representing and promoting God. They needed to enter the new kingdom that was ushered in by Jesus. That meant a new set of friends.

They would be joining efforts with and opening their purses to fishermen, tax collectors, and women of low repute. They could no longer hide among socially respectable teachers and scribes. Nicodemus didn't mind the teachings of Jesus. They rang true to him. He lurked in the shadows and met Jesus at night because he wasn't ready to associate with the people of Jesus. He didn't want to be mistaken for one of them.[1]

Many would-be disciples today find themselves in the same boat. They are attracted to the teachings of Jesus. The Bible is very important to them. They even bear the name Christian, but they wish to have nothing to do with Christ's body. They want to be part of God's activity, on the side of truth, and on the winning side of world history. But they don't want to join a revolutionary people movement.

So they work hard to study Scripture faithfully, pray regularly, raise their children diligently, show kindness to all people, and even attend Christian rallies, conventions, and Bible study groups. Yet they will not commit to a local body. They want no part in the people movement Jesus set into motion. They dabble around the margins, but never cross into the center.[2] Jesus met people like this. He knew them all too well. But doing these sorts of things isn't enough, even if they are right and good. It surprised people when Jesus said that such things aren't enough. Allow me to paraphrase their sentiments in Matthew 7:21–22:

"But Lord, didn't we read our Bibles religiously? Didn't we give our tithes to humanitarian causes? Didn't we attend every Christian moms, dads, and students rally within driving distance? Didn't we turn our eyes away from pornography and smutty novels? Weren't we model citizens at work and in our neighborhoods? We boycotted every corporation that propagated falsehood. We signed every petition to oust immoral people from positions of influence. We subscribed to every religious LISTSERV and drank from every fountain of contemporary Christian wisdom. We've liked, shared, and even shed tears at every story of life transformation that crossed our news feed. Doesn't any of this count for something?"

"Very truly I tell you," Jesus said to the sincere Pharisee, "no one can see the kingdom of God unless they are born again" (John 3:3).

The change Jesus brings is more drastic than moral reform. Disciples do not find themselves on a solitary journey of finding oneself by

1. The next time we encounter Nicodemus is when he defends Jesus' right to be heard. At that point the other Pharisees respond by associating him with people from Galilee (John 7:50–52). They don't point out a flaw in his logic; they apply social pressure by asking, essentially, are you *one of them* or *one of us*?

2. Of course there are also many believers who are committed to regular involvement in church programming, but have not entered into a kingdom-centered life together with fellow members. Obviously, the problem in such cases is not that they aren't part of a church, but *how* they are a part of the church. They are members of a sort, but they aren't kingdom-centered members.

finding God. God has already found us. He came in the flesh and found a bunch of aimless sheep, wandering around in an effort to find him. Jesus gathered those sheep and bound them to himself and to one another. He promised that as they continued to gather he would continue to dwell in their midst, he would give them his Spirit, and he would send them throughout the earth in order to gather even more scattered sheep into his fold—his body which seeks first his kingdom.

Disciples as the Better Place

Let's say that at this point, perhaps, you agree: there is no such thing as Lone Ranger Christianity. You recognize that being a Christian means being part of a church. What impact does *being a better place* have on the daily walk of a disciple who is part of a church? Here are just a few examples.

(1) *Disciples stop thinking of "I can do all things through Christ who strengthens me" as just an individual confession.* God strengthens us through each other. We need to think and act not only as if God is an invisible force by our side, but also as if God is visibly with us *through the body of Christ*. We need to move from a mentality that asks, "Can I do this with God's help?" to one that asks, "Should we do this with the resources God has given us as a body?"

It was the Apostle Paul who wrote, "I can do all things through Christ who strengthens me" (Phil 4:13). He was the same person who asked churches to give generously to one another and to other churches in need. It was Paul, again, who taught that every member of the body of Christ has been empowered by God precisely in order to meet the needs of other members of the body. Paul did not write or operate as if each believer had an all-sufficient direct line to God. He taught that God's power works among us through one another.

It is worth noting that Scripture uses a specific kind of language to talk about God's power at work in his people. In 1 Corinthians 12–14, for example, Paul uses the term *charism*, which means gift, grace, or favor. God bestows grace upon each member so the body can function properly and lead a healthy life of love.

In Ephesians 4, he uses the language of gift. When Christ ascended on high, he showered gifts upon the church as a celebration of his victory over sin and death: "The gifts he gave were that some would be apostles, some prophets, some evangelists, some pastors and teachers, to equip the saints for the work of ministry, for building up the body of Christ" (vv. 11–12). These gifts are *people*! They are people who unify the body of Christ and help it mature into Christ. God is the source of all these good gifts, and so we give him all glory. But we can't divorce God's favor from its human hands and feet. Those hands and feet *are* God's gift.

(2) *Disciples strive to live, at all times, in line with the new socioeconomic order made possible by Christ.* According to Scripture, this is a life of *koinonia*. This Greek word is often translated as "fellowship." Though fellowship is most often associated with socializing, it means much more. It means sharing things in common with Christ and fellow disciples. For instance, we share faith and the gospel. We share in Christ's sufferings and life. We share finances and possessions. Yet, we don't share life in common merely because it is practical or efficient. It's not simply a way to meet needs or fix the world. We share life in common because God's kingdom is a life of joy and generosity in shared abundance. We do so because we are privileged to embrace, display, and proclaim that kingdom.

Joyfully sharing possessions was basic to the early church's common life (Acts 2:42–47; 4:32–34). Though such sharing can be structured in a variety of ways, it should always reflect that our possessions are gifts from God and assets of his kingdom people. Even our free time gives us opportunities to serve fellow believers and display shared abundance. As disciples, we reject the world's lie that we deserve our excess and that we are entitled to chase after ever-increasing standards of living.

Shared life also means involving the body of Christ in important decisions. Our decisions aren't just ours. Choices that involve a significant portion of our time and resources profoundly impact the wider body. It is only fitting that those people who are impacted by our decisions have a say in them. My decision to adopt a particular kind of dog may make my family happy, but it may also make it impossible for fellow believers with allergies to spend time in my house. God has provided the body with all the people it needs to make wise decisions. What's more, when the body is gathered in Jesus' name, God's Spirit is present to guide us into truth (Matt 18:18–20; John 16:13). In the world, independence is a sign of maturity; in the church, *interdependence* points to God's kingdom.

(3) *Disciples move beyond the question "What can I do to show people God's love?" to "How can we as a body display God's kingdom by loving each other the way God loves us?"* This is the most loving thing we can do for our neighbor. Like any caring human, we can honor our neighbor by

meeting this or that need. But as someone who seeks first God's kingdom, we trust that God's plan to draw people to himself through our love for one another reflects his infinite wisdom. It's how he has chosen to embrace all people in his love.

The church of which I am a part encounters needs on a regular basis. We strive first to make sure that all needs within our body are met. We don't wait until people's lives fall apart and then bail one another out. Instead, we share enough life and possessions in common that things seldom fall apart financially. Having done so, we usually have plenty to share with those beyond the body.

When any of us encounters an opportunity to share God's abundance with someone outside the body, we bring it before the body as well. In most of these cases, each of us as individuals could have met the need ourselves. But when we give as individuals, we find that people too often respond by being grateful to us as individuals. They usually try to give something back as soon as possible in order to even the scales. Giving as a church, on the other hand, encourages people to give thanks and glory to God. They interpret the gift as God reaching into their life in a way they didn't expect. The member who delivers the gift on behalf of the body is then able to testify how this sort of thing is common at church, how all needs are generously met, and how blessed it is to be a part of God's kingdom.

The kind of discipleship discussed in this chapter presupposes a certain kind of church community. It presupposes a people whose life is structured in such a way that questions can be raised, opportunities discussed, and doubts expressed. It presupposes members who are willing to listen to one another, wait for one another, and respond to one another. Learning those skills is very much a part of Christian maturity. They are, indeed, the evidence or fruit of God's Spirit.

Learning these skills is a tough task. We usually need help as we learn. God has provided such help through his people. What forms does that help take? What kinds of leaders and structures help the church mature?

16

Leadership

"JESUS PREACHED THE KINGDOM," people commonly observe, "but we're stuck with the church." Hopefully I've convinced you that pitting God's kingdom against God's church is a bad idea. But this raises an important point: Jesus didn't leave behind detailed blueprints for how to structure church life. Instead he gave us a vision of the kingdom and the power of his Spirit. But the Holy Spirit didn't give us a blueprint either. How then should we organize church life?

Christian traditions all throughout history have answered this question in different ways. Many contemporary authors have also spelled out how they think church life should be structured, some based on Scripture, others on sociology. I don't feel the need to repeat or critique their thoughts. Diverse approaches are necessary to help congregations discern how to display God's kingdom in the specific situations in which they find themselves.

My goal is to look at what Scripture says about church leadership and bring that into conversation with different Christian approaches to a better place. I am not *prescribing* how churches should structure their leadership. We're not ready for that (yet). Instead, I'm *describing* what functions church leaders should serve according to Scripture and asking what approach to a better place lines up best with Scripture's teaching.

Considering the Options

Heaven-centered and world-centered churches gravitate toward certain forms of leadership. For example, when churches focus on preparing

131

people for a better place somewhere else (heaven centered), their leaders concentrate on getting people into the church and getting them ready for heaven. Their agenda is quite concrete and measurable.

They have to determine exactly what "preparation" looks like. They have to distinguish between who is prepared and who is not. They must strive to discern the most efficient way to get people from point A to point B. Once someone has arrived, leaders serve to keep them in good standing and involve them in the task of bringing others along as well. This being the case, the newest members receive the bulk of the attention.

When churches focus on making this world a better place (world centered), their leaders must discern what is wrong in the world around them and which of these wrongs their church is best suited to make right. They have to be strong in the areas of assessment and management.

Good leaders in this model ask questions like, What are the needs? What are the church's human and material resources? How can people and resources be coordinated so as to maximize their need-meeting potential? Has a particular need been met? If so, should the church move on to address another need? What if a particular need never goes away? Should the church stick only to goals that are achievable? With this approach, those in need receive the most energy and attention.

These visions of the church's responsibility call forth specific sorts of leaders. Since the goal of the heaven-centered view is to draw people in and keep them in, attractive and magnetic leadership is ideal. Leaders need to be creative and adaptive in order to keep people connected over the long haul. The ability to equip members to replicate the work of drawing and keeping people is equally important.

Since the focus of the world-centered view is identifying, prioritizing, and meeting needs, its leadership style is highly administrative. The ability to evaluate, plan, and execute is central. Leaders need a reliable strategy for dealing with competing voices. Not everyone will gravitate toward the same set of needs. Some people will question the church's priorities when their perceived needs don't receive equal attention. Since this model requires administrating both material and human assets, it also benefits from a certain degree of attractional and magnetic leadership.

What would change if the church's first priority were to be the better place that God has already begun? What if the church's mission were to embrace, display, and proclaim the kingdom? What kind of leadership would the kingdom-centered view require? Does it matter that the church is called *to be* a certain way and not *to do* a certain thing? That depends, of course, on *what* the church is supposed *to be* like.

Leading Toward the Kingdom

Remember Jesus' focus on describing what the kingdom is like. He has already shown us what kind of people we are supposed to be. We are supposed to be *like the kingdom*. We must receive the kingdom humbly, like a child. It is a kingdom in which first is last and last is first, where the great are least and the least are great, where worldly wealth and power do not confer status and are often liabilities, where every member is important and greater honor is given to the least honorable so that there may be equality (1 Cor 12:24–25).

It is a kingdom that unifies through diversity, operates by the wisdom of the cross, and has only one head: Christ. The kingdom is empowered and guided by God's Spirit, which has been given to all members. Each member needs all others because God organized the body in such a way that each part would be incomplete without all the others.

This kingdom is unlike all earthly kingdoms. It is little wonder that it calls forth a form of leadership unlike theirs. When we look at the New Testament teaching on leadership, it is interesting to observe what is and is not there.

What We Don't See on Leadership in the New Testament

One does not find, first of all, a detailed job description. Outside of Ephesians 4, which I discuss below, we are told very little about what leaders are supposed to *do*. We are told that they must be able to teach and gently correct opponents (2 Tim 2:24–25) and that their function involves providing oversight (1 Pet 5:2; Heb 13:17).

We are never told that this means casting a vision for the body or making decisions on its behalf. On the contrary, when important decisions need to be made in congregations like Corinth, the Apostle Paul instructs the body to decide and act together. Even though that church was terribly dysfunctional, the apostle never addresses leaders directly by telling them to do their job or by singling them out in any way. Instead, he defers to the discernment of the wider body (1 Cor 5:1–13; 11:13).

Likewise, Paul repeatedly encourages the church in Philippi to "be of one mind." It can do so by having the mind of Christ and by following the example of the apostles (Phil 1:27; 2:2–5; 3:15–17; 4:2). Paul never instructs all the members to get behind the vision of their leaders. Why? Because their shared Messiah and mission unites them—not their leaders.

This does not mean that leaders will not play an important role in decision-making. All members play a vital role, and those who are called to be examples should be clearly seen and heard. Community-minded decision-making doesn't happen magically. Order and process are required, and that means leadership. But we should be careful not to assume that kingdom leadership, like worldly leadership, involves the power to make decisions and impose them upon others. That framework is central to what it means to "lord over" and "rule over," which is strictly off-limits for church leaders (Mark 10:42–43; 1 Pet 5:3).

We just do not find any of the attributes of "take-charge," worldly leaders commended in the New Testament. We are never told that church leaders should be attractional, charismatic, decisive, persuasive, commanding, accomplished, or even educated. Despite the fact that he embodied many of these attributes, the Apostle Paul publicly renounced them. To him this was necessary so people would see what Christ has done and not what he was doing (1 Cor 2:1–5).

What We Do See on Leadership in the New Testament

We do find many Scriptures that emphasize how leaders must serve others rather than control them (Luke 22:25–27; John 13). We also hear that leaders must be examples to the body (Heb 13:7; 1 Pet 5:3). Since the body must embrace, display, and proclaim the kingdom, its leaders should *embrace* the kingdom like a gift, *display* it in their home life, work life, and community life, and *proclaim* it to others every chance they get.

The desirable attributes in elders and deacons are revealing. They are nearly the opposite of what we see in decisive leaders who step in, take charge, and get results. Leaders are supposed to be calm, hospitable, gentle, peaceable, patient, kind, self-controlled, consistent, and free from the love of money and desire for greatness (1 Tim 3; Titus 1).[1] These

---

1. It is telling that many of the characteristics of false teachers listed in 2 Timothy 3:2–5 are the exact opposite of the qualifications for elders and deacons. False teachers are lovers of themselves, money, and pleasure. They are arrogant boasters who hold an outward form of godliness that denies its power. Yet these are exactly what we find among many magnetic, attractional personalities.

attributes resemble the fruit of the Spirit: love, joy, peace, patience, kindness, goodness, faithfulness, gentleness, and self-control (Gal 5:22–23).

This resemblance is not coincidental. God wants these same qualities in all of his people. They are also exactly what we would expect to find if leaders were not called to get something done but to lead others by example in being the kind of people whose life together reflects God's kingdom. God's kingdom is not a social or functional hierarchy; it is a fellowship of equal but distinct members.

Growing into Christ

Leading as an equal does not come naturally. Worldly leadership relies on the extraordinary ability of superior people. It elevates exceptional people, gives them power, trusts that they will use their power responsibly for the good of the organization, and expects them to get things done. Quite simply, this is not how Jesus framed leadership. The Apostle Paul's most extensive teaching on leaders, which is the closest thing we have to a job description, also pushes in the opposition direction:

> So Christ himself gave the apostles, the prophets, the evangelists, the pastors and teachers, to equip his people for works of service, so that the body of Christ may be built up until we all reach unity in the faith and in the knowledge of the Son of God and become mature, attaining to the whole measure of the fullness of Christ. Then we will no longer be infants, tossed back and forth by the waves, and blown here and there by every wind of teaching and by the cunning and craftiness of people in their deceitful scheming. Instead, speaking the truth in love, we will grow to become in every respect the mature body of him who is the head, that is, Christ. From him the whole body, joined and held together by every supporting ligament, grows and builds itself up in love, as each part does its work. (Eph 4:11–16, NIV)

Leadership in the church is not a purely natural institution. To Paul, it is a divine gift. Christ gave leaders to the church so they might equip other members for works of service. The congregation doesn't elevate the leaders so they can get the work done; leaders elevate the members so they can do the work of the body. And the nature of that work, according to this passage, is quite revealing. Leaders equip God's people in multiple ways:

- In the work of service

- In building the body of Christ

- In unity of faith and knowledge

- In maturity

- In the fullness of Christ

- In Christ who is our head

- In building itself up in love

Paul is keen to stress that Christ is the head. Because we've been raised in a broken world, it's tempting to think of the apostles, pastors, and teachers as heads of the body. Instead, these people are given to the church by its head in order to help all body parts do the ministry of the body. Leaders are given as gifts to build up the body so it may display the fullness of Christ—a life of love. That is their particular ministry.

Put differently, church leaders help all members lead in their areas of giftedness so the whole body might reflect Christ and his kingdom. They serve the body by helping it grow into the better place God has called the church to be. There is no other endgame. Paul assumes that if the church becomes a place of love that reflects Christ's fullness, then it has accomplished its most fundamental task. Neither the lost nor the needy of this world take precedence. Fellow members of Christ's body take precedence.

This kind of leadership makes sense within the kingdom-centered paradigm we see in Scripture. It makes sense if God seeks to bless all nations through his people by making the church's life together his better place in this world. Paul does not commission leaders—not even evangelists—to attract people. The body's mutual love and reflection of Christ attracts people. This Ephesians passage just doesn't make sense if the mission of God's people centered on making this world a better place. Fixing the world isn't even on the radar. Being what God has called the church to be takes center stage and we need leaders who will lead us in it.

17

Fellowship

FOR A CHURCH'S LIFE to display God's kingdom, its members must commit to the practice of fellowship. In chapter 15, I noted that fellowship means more than socializing. It means sharing a life in common. In that chapter I focused on the economic dimensions of fellowship: how we share our financial and material resources. In this chapter, I focus on sharing life in common—being together, truly together.

New Testament Togetherness

A host of Christian practices require members to gather together regularly. The "one another" passages of the New Testament give us a good picture of what that looks like:

- Accept one another (Rom 15:7).

- Agree with one another (1 Cor 1:10; 3:13).

- Be kind to one another (1 Thess 5:15).

- Be subject to one another (Eph 5:21).

- Bear with one another (Col 3:13).

- Carry one another's burdens (Gal 6:2).

- Encourage one another (Heb 3:13; 1 Thess 4:18).

- Fellowship with one another (1 John 1:7).

- Forgive one another (Eph 4:32).

- Love one another (John 13:34–35, 15:12, 17; 1 John 4:7; 2 John 1:5).

- Live in harmony with one another (Rom 12:16).

- Offer hospitality to one another (1 Pet 4:9).

- Serve one another (Gal 5:13).

- Show equal concern for one another (1 Cor 12:25).

- Speak to one another with psalms, hymns, and spiritual songs (Eph 5:19).

- Teach and admonish one another (Col 3:16).

- Wait for one another before breaking bread (1 Cor 11:33).

The distinguishing feature of the "one another" practices is reciprocity. These are not practices that a few people do on behalf of the whole body. They are how *all* members relate to one another. It's not enough for leaders to accept the members; members need to accept their leaders and all other members. It's not enough for the clergy to forgive the sins of those who come to confession; members need to forgive one another. Jesus warns that those who fail to forgive one another will fail to receive God's forgiveness (Matt 6:14–15). This would be a harsh punishment if broken relationships within the body didn't undermine the church's primary responsibility. But since that responsibility entails displaying God's kingdom, the punishment is appropriate.

Many of the "one another" practices require the genuine intimacy of life together. Paul had to instruct believers in Corinth to "wait for one another" because rich members began feasting during church gatherings without waiting for poor members. Sharing meals was, and still is, an intimate practice. It is often said "we are *what we eat*"; even more so, we are *who we eat with*. Jesus was called a "friend of sinners" because he ate with them. He wasn't content to preach at them from the hilltops; he made a point of dining with them. The practice of hospitality involves welcoming Christian brothers and sisters—even the unpopular ones—into the intimate space of one's immediate family.

Togetherness Today

These "one another" commands are not simply a matter of first-century or even small church culture. They reflect God's design for human life and flourishing. The ancient laws of Israel pointed in the same direction.

Once the kingdom had begun and Christ had broken down the walls that separate people, fellowship was the natural expression of the early church's newfound joy and life. It's where believers most tangibly experienced the kingdom.

In the early church, many Christians still lived under the authority of unbelieving rulers, employers, and family members. For them, gathering together with the body was the only time they truly experienced the newness of God's kingdom. They couldn't wait to get together. They looked forward to serving one another and being served, encouraging one another and being encouraged, teaching others and being taught. The lowly looked forward to being raised up. Women, children, slaves, and ethnic minorities looked forward to being treated with equal dignity.

The kingdom cannot mean any less for us today. We still live in a world in which people regularly experience discrimination at work, school, and home. We still live in a world where race, gender, age, pedigree, and net worth confer privilege and deny access. People still yearn to be part of a community that appreciates them for who they are, welcomes them into a life of flourishing that revolves around something bigger than themselves, and includes others who are not like them. People long to be at the center of the meaning of world history despite their inadequacies. They long to experience God's kingdom in real life.

What would it look like for a church to fellowship like that? What sorts of structures would foster the genuine togetherness of God's kingdom? Some of it can be experienced during a large worship service, but not all of it. Midweek Bible studies or small groups might fill some other gaps, but they can't do it all either.

In 1 Corinthians 12, Paul talks about members who suffer together and rejoice together. Where do people suffer and rejoice today? Are church buildings the places where people do that? If not, where? Are God's people together in *those* places? Do they truly share in one another's joy and pain? Where this is the case, is it experienced by the many or the few? Is it happening among pockets of friends who are a lot alike, just as it happens in the world? Or is it happening beyond the comfortable confines of race, gender, age, status, and social compatibility?

Churches have long found small group structures to be a helpful way to foster intimate fellowship. For small groups to display the better place of God's kingdom, they will have to move beyond optional *a la carte* programming. Small groups should be integral to church membership. They are not merely ways of attracting, assimilating, and retaining members. Their goal should be to embrace and display Christ's wonderful gift of new life in community with God and one another.

For this new life together to display God's new creation, small groups must strive to reflect the diversity of the kingdom as much as possible. They should at least be a reflection of the wider body's diversity. They should not be affinity groups—people who are easy to love because they are just like us (Matt 5:46–47). That kind of relationship only mirrors back to the world a love that it already knows.

Since proximity is central to togetherness, church groups should also be mindful of location. It is difficult to rejoice together over a victory at work on Tuesday when one has to drive thirty minutes each way. It's easy to pray together for a sudden need when one's church family lives right around the corner. Close proximity also makes it convenient to lend a car in a pinch, borrow a ladder, or help a sister in Christ study for a big exam.

Just Another Fad?

At this point, you might have some suspicions. Is this just another "community" fad? Am I just trying to swing the pendulum away from big impersonal churches and toward small intimate churches? Sure, you might be thinking, every once in a while we need to be reminded not to make too big a deal about size and to remember the value of small intimate communities. That's all well and good, but what about the command to grow? What happens when we grow up and out? Being faithful means being healthy, right? And if we are healthy, won't we grow?

You might have read some of the many sociological studies that examine how relationships change when the number of members increases. These studies have consistently shown that there are major shifts in a community when its membership reaches certain numbers. Usually these studies include recommendations about how to change your organization's structure in order to help you overcome the forty people barrier, the 200 barrier, 450, 800, and so on.[1] Those structural changes are only natural; they are the protocol to follow when membership reaches a certain size. If we assume that we're supposed to grow, and with growth comes necessary adaptations, then the right and obedient thing to do is

---

1. Tim Keller analyzes the impact of church size on church leadership and structure in "Leadership and Church Size Dynamics."

adapt. According to this logic, my concerns about "big churches" likely seem naïve.

One might also observe that small churches are not necessarily faithful. Different people simply have different preferences. Some prefer the intimacy of smaller churches. Such contexts enable certain people to grow and flourish. But they shouldn't judge bigger churches. Many people thrive in bigger churches. Why does it matter? There are plenty of options for everyone. It's just a matter of preference.

It is impossible to deny the sociological implications of growth. It is true that organizations that seek to grow will have to adapt or die when they reach certain head counts. The cumulative data to this effect is overwhelming. But we must take care that the tail doesn't wag the dog. What are the facts that rightly guide faithfulness?

God's mission centers on welcoming people into the better place begun by Jesus. We do this by incorporating them into communities whose life together embraces, displays, and proclaims God's kingdom. That being the case, we are not free to change the nature of those communities for any reason, not even sociological "fact." If numerical growth demands a different kind of community and a different kind of leader than Jesus exemplified and authorized, then we have three options:

1. We can leave Jesus' teaching about community behind and allow sociology to guide us into new forms of church for which Scripture offers little guidance.

2. We can plant new churches whenever we get too large to conform to Jesus' teaching about community.

3. We can find ways to adapt our life together in such a way that takes sociological constraints seriously while keeping Jesus' teaching about the kingdom as our authoritative guide.

Option 1 is flat-out dangerous. If the church's new life together is part of the gospel message as it was for the Apostle Paul—the new creation and new humanity—than seriously tinkering with the church's DNA means tinkering with the gospel. I don't see why that would be any less of a concern for us today than it was for Paul in the first century. I do not presume to speak for God, but a word of caution is certainly in order.

That leaves us with options 2 and 3. We have no biblical word on what apostolic churches did when they reached a size limit that prevented them from ordering their life together to reflect Jesus' revelation of the kingdom. Planting new churches would certainly work. Adapting our structures to include churches within churches or networks of groups within one church may also work.

What is most important is that the visible body of Christ gathers and shares life in ways that participate firsthand in the new humanity and new creation of God's kingdom. We must baptize people now, like they baptized people in Paul's day, into a church body among which there is neither Jew nor Gentile, slave nor free, male nor female—where diverse people are truly one in Christ Jesus (Gal 3:27–29). We must baptize them into a body where every member is equipped to do the work of ministry according to the Spirit given them in order to build up the body of Christ in love—each member doing its part—until it reaches fullness in Christ. We must baptize them into a body in which the various forms of ministering to "one another" in Christ have become their new life rhythm.

If we are not baptizing people into a body like this, then we may be embracing, displaying, and proclaiming a sophisticated "sociological" substitute for the kingdom of God. That is not an exchange we should be willing to make. Scripture is too clear about the breadth and depth of fellowship in Christ. "Growth" that happens outside or in spite of that depth of intimacy is suspicious at best.

Fellowship is God's Gift

Developing and maintaining this kind of fellowship can seem like a lot of work. Intimate relationships require time, energy, and devotion. Again, these observations are true. That's the "bad news," if you want to call it that.

The opportunity for new life in Christ and the better place he has created is good news. And it gets even better. We don't have to create these relationships. God has already forged the new humanity. Our task is to embrace and enjoy God's good gift. Our job isn't to make relationships grow. It's to have faith that God has already accomplished that task and then plan our lives accordingly. If we don't have time to truly share our lives with fellow believers, then our root problem is faith. If we don't make time to truly love and prioritize one another in devoted Christian fellowship, we don't really believe that we have been raised to newness of life together.

If some of us feel alone in our homes, it is because we don't really believe and act as if we have been adopted into a new family and made friends of one other. If some of us feel miserable while working on large house projects or navigating through difficult struggles, it is because we don't really believe and act as if our homes and struggles truly belong to one another. If churches have to farm out the discipleship of their youth to parachurch organizations, perhaps we don't really believe that Christ has given his body all the gifts it needs to meet our needs. If several of our members have found that the best way to pass time is to stare at and manipulate miniature handheld devices, maybe it's because our imaginations have been captured by a reality more interesting, worthwhile, and demanding than their experience of God's kingdom.

If those who work among the powers and principalities find their most profound fulfillment through their nine-to-five contributions to world betterment, it is because we don't really believe and act as if the old order is truly passing away and that the new order has truly begun. If any of us regards our life together as tiresome, tedious work rather than an energizing and life-transforming gift, it is because we don't really believe and act as if together we are the firstfruits of God's new creation, the new world on the way, the very thing the prophets longed for and the angels wondered about. These experiences expose the unsettling fact that our life together in God's kingdom is secondary to something else. Whatever our life truly revolves around is the actual center of our identity. What a hopeless situation, indeed. And for many of us, that is our situation.

Imagine instead the light and easy yoke that Jesus offers us. Imagine being part of a church where people don't feel lonely because they find themselves in regular fellowship with friends in Christ.

Imagine being part of a church where those working on big projects or struggling through major problems don't have to constantly beg for help because brothers and sisters in Christ check in daily to see how things are going and offer help before being asked.

Imagine a body in which we don't have to plan special events for our youth because they are already busy doing special things throughout the week with brothers and sisters, aunts and uncles in the faith.

Imagine a life together that is bustling with such meaningful activity that members don't need to aimlessly search through Netflix or Hulu trying to find yet another show that can capture their interests and imaginations for a short time, only to leave them feeling empty again when it's over.

Imagine a world in which kids don't have to watch endless Disney Channel reruns or scan through various app stores looking for free games to help them deal with their insufferable boredom.

Imagine members who can't wait to get home from work so they can see what everyone at church is doing that night and to hear about what they've been doing all day.

Imagine us not caring whether we will be serving someone, watching shows, or playing games together because we've learned to find enjoyment in doing what others enjoy and serving together whatever the task may be.

Imagine what it would be like if we renounced the idol of personal preferences, likes and dislikes, which, according to our culture, makes us unique. Imagine a world in which life in the body no longer interrupts our real lives because it has become the primary rhythm of our lives. Imagine instead that our life together in kingdom fellowship is our true life which gets interrupted by jobs, chores, and the need for sleep.

This is what God asks of his people because it's precisely what he's made of us. And it's the kind of fellowship that a lost world desperately needs to find.

18

Family Relationships

IN THE WESTERN WORLD, what makes a family appears to be up for grabs. The ABC sitcom *Modern Family* nicely represents some of today's diverse options. Jay, the patriarch of the family, is a white man remarried to a younger Latina woman. She brings a young teenager from a previous marriage into their newly blended family, and they soon have a child of their own together. Jay's adult children from his first marriage make up the two other families in the show. His daughter, Claire, is a stay-at-home mom (for the first few seasons) with a working husband and three kids. Jay's son Mitchell marries a man and they adopt a Vietnamese girl.

Though this diversity marks a significant departure from *The Waltons* and *Little House on the Prairie*, it captures several key aspects of the contemporary family landscape, including different ages, ethnicities, and genders. Though some of these pairings are less common in practice than they are on the big screen, divorce, remarriage, and the blending of families is quite familiar. What all these different families share is a strong sense of solidarity: the people you choose to build a family with become the center of your world. Family comes first.

Such prioritizing of the family is not significantly different in today's church. When it comes to the place of family in our lives, Christian counsel often sounds like airline safety protocol: if there is a loss of cabin pressure, put your own mask on first, then that of the child next to you, and finally the mask of anyone else. In the same way, spiritual advisors often insist that people should put their own needs first, then their family, and finally the church. They want to make sure that God's people don't get so lost in service to the church that they become workaholics who neglect themselves and their families.

Such wisdom is practical and sometimes a helpful corrective, but it is not the way of Jesus. Seeking God's kingdom *first* means making local church life our number one priority. This is not because the church family is always so great, but because the local church is central to God's kingdom mission.

What does this mean? Does it mean we have to neglect ourselves or our biological family? We instinctively want to answer that question with a resounding "No!" even before we've read what Scripture has to say on the subject. But as with other questions, we need to let Scripture speak.

Actually, when it comes to family, the New Testament is surprising and puzzling. We see passages that would seem to support competing answers to the question of familial neglect. Some imply radical separation from one's family; others presume radical faithfulness to one's family. A brief overview of these passages will put our topic into biblical perspective.

Radical Separation

More than most believers realize, the New Testament appears to challenge the basic tenets of family-friendly churches. Consider the following passages:

> "Who are my mother and my brothers?" And looking at those who sat around him, he said, "Here are my mother and my brothers! Whoever does the will of God is my brother and sister and mother." (Mark 3:33–35)

> Then his mother and his brothers came to him, but they could not reach him because of the crowd. And he was told, "Your mother and your brothers are standing outside, wanting to see you." But he said to them, "My mother and my brothers are those who hear the word of God and do it." (Luke 8:19–21)

> Truly I tell you, there is no one who has left house or brothers or sisters or mother or father or children or fields, for my sake and for the sake of the good news, who will not receive a hundredfold now in this age—houses, brothers and sisters, mothers and

children, and fields with persecutions—and in the age to come eternal life. (Mark 10:29–30)

Call no one your father on earth, for you have one Father—the one in heaven. (Matt 23:9)

Do not think that I have come to bring peace to the earth; I have not come to bring peace, but a sword. For I have come to set a man against his father, and a daughter against her mother, and a daughter-in-law against her mother-in-law; and one's foes will be members of one's own household. Whoever loves father or mother more than me is not worthy of me; and whoever loves son or daughter more than me is not worthy of me. (Matt 10:34–37)

To another he said, "Follow me." But he said, "Lord, first let me go and bury my father." But Jesus said to him, "Let the dead bury their own dead; but as for you, go and proclaim the kingdom of God." (Luke 9:59–60)

Whoever comes to me and does not hate father and mother, wife and children, brothers and sisters, yes, and even life itself, cannot be my disciple. (Luke 14:26).

Those who marry will experience distress in this life, and I would spare you that. I mean, brothers and sisters, the appointed time has grown short; from now on, let even those who have wives be as though they had none, and those who mourn as though they were not mourning, and those who rejoice as though they were not rejoicing, and those who buy as though they had no possessions, and those who deal with the world as though they had no dealings with it. For the present form of this world is passing away. I want you to be free from anxieties. The unmarried man is anxious about the affairs of the Lord, how to please the Lord; but the married man is anxious about the affairs of the world, how to please his wife, and his interests are divided. And the unmarried woman and the virgin are anxious about the affairs of the Lord, so that they may be holy in body and spirit; but the married woman is anxious about the affairs of the world, how to please her husband. I say this for your own benefit, not to put any restraint upon you, but to promote good order and unhindered devotion to the Lord. (1 Cor 7:28–35)

> For in the resurrection they neither marry nor are given in marriage, but are like angels in heaven. (Matt 22:30)

If these were the only passages, our position would be clear. Christ has called us to break our biological ties and avoid marrying and forming new ones. God has given us a new family in place of our old one.

Radical Faithfulness

But those are not the only passages on the subject. Several passages appear to pull in the opposite direction.

> From the beginning of creation, "God made them male and female." "For this reason a man shall leave his father and mother and be joined to his wife, and the two shall become one flesh." So they are no longer two, but one flesh. Therefore what God has joined together, let no one separate. (Mark 10:6–9)

> Because of cases of sexual immorality, each man should have his own wife and each woman her own husband. The husband should give to his wife her conjugal rights, and likewise the wife to her husband. For the wife does not have authority over her own body, but the husband does; likewise the husband does not have authority over his own body, but the wife does. Do not deprive one another except perhaps by agreement for a set time, to devote yourselves to prayer. (1 Cor 7:2–5)

> Be subject to one another out of reverence for Christ. Wives, be subject to your husbands as you are to the Lord. For the husband is the head of the wife just as Christ is the head of the church, the body of which he is the Savior. Just as the church is subject to Christ, so also wives ought to be, in everything, to their husbands. Husbands, love your wives, just as Christ loved the church and gave himself up for her, in order to make her holy by cleansing her with the washing of water by the word, so as to present the church to himself in splendor, without a spot or wrinkle or anything of the kind—yes, so that she may be holy and without blemish. In the same way, husbands should love their wives as they do their own bodies. He who loves his wife loves himself. For no one ever hates his own body, but he nourishes and tenderly cares for it, just as Christ does for the church. (Eph 5:21–29)

Let marriage be held in honor by all, and let the marriage bed be kept undefiled; for God will judge fornicators and adulterers. (Heb 13:4)

Children, obey your parents in the Lord, for this is right. "Honor your father and mother"—this is the first commandment with a promise: "so that it may be well with you and you may live long on the earth." And, fathers, do not provoke your children to anger, but bring them up in the discipline and instruction of the Lord. (Eph 6:1–4)

Children, obey your parents in everything, for this is your acceptable duty in the Lord. (Col 3:20)

If a widow has children or grandchildren, they should first learn their religious duty to their own family and make some repayment to their parents; for this is pleasing in God's sight. (1 Tim 5:4)

Whoever does not provide for relatives, and especially for family members, has denied the faith and is worse than an unbeliever. (1 Tim 5:8)

These verses make clear that being in Christ also means upholding marriage, being radically faithful to spouses, honoring parents, raising children in the Lord, and providing for the financial needs of one's biological kin.

The New Testament thus appears to be sending mixed signals about family. On the one hand, the family cannot come before God's kingdom. On the other hand, we must remain faithfully devoted to our families. Some have resolved this tension by suggesting that there are two Christian paths. Those who can handle it should dissolve blood ties and live radical single lives of unhindered devotion to the Lord. Those who cannot stomach this should get married, live a family-centered life, and seek the kingdom less fervently.

This approach has its merits. Both Jesus and Paul invited people to a single life even as they conceded that most people will not accept it (Matt 19:10–12; 1 Cor 7:7–40). Those who embrace singleness are certainly freer in many ways to pursue the kingdom with their time, energy, and resources. But this approach does not go far enough. It implies that those who marry are off the hook for radical discipleship and may seek God's kingdom second rather than first.

Jesus, the Family Man

We get a fuller picture when we carefully consider the example of Jesus. His teachings about family are best understood against the background of the life he lived.

- At a young age Jesus informed his parents that God's will was his first priority (Luke 2:42–52).

- Jesus' brothers did not believe his message (John 7:5).

- Jesus snubbed his family when they tried to restrain his ministry and told his followers that those who do God's will are his true family (Mark 3:21–35).

- Jesus' innermost circle of relationships comprised those who embraced the kingdom (Luke 9:1–6).

- Jesus had intimate familial relationships with disciples wherever he went (John 11; 13:23).

- Before being arrested and killed, Jesus spent his final moments among his closest followers (Mark 14:33).

- Jesus included his mother in his work and, from the cross, appointed one of his disciples to look after her (John 19:26–27).

- Non-family members took it upon themselves to bury Jesus (John 19:38–40).

- After he ascended, Jesus' mother and brothers integrated among his disciples (Acts 1:14).

- Jesus' brother James became a prominent leader in the Jerusalem church (Acts 15:13), perhaps because Jesus personally approached him after the resurrection (1 Cor 15:7).

This snapshot of Jesus' life gives us a fuller picture of how Jesus viewed family. He definitely viewed his family as being *more than* blood relatives. His family included those who embraced God's kingdom. Yet this did not mean leaving his biological family behind altogether. Rather, Jesus' concept of family was broad enough to include fellow citizens of

God's kingdom. When his mother and brothers invoked family ties to trump his kingdom work, Jesus pushed back hard. But he didn't try to push them away. He honored them enough to present them a true picture of God's priorities. How else could they see his kingdom in action?

Jesus also maintained a cordial relationship with his family, even as he refused to limit familial relationships to biological kin. Jesus' mother remained a steady presence in his life, and his brothers seem to have come around. Although he pursued economic independence and forged a new life with his disciples, he did not alienate his family altogether. But since his new life revolved around the kingdom and its people, anyone who wished to play a major role in his life had to enter the wider circle of his kingdom family. This is exactly what happened. Mary became family with John (John 19:26–27), and Jesus' brothers eventually joined his disciples (Acts 1:14). Their unity as a family was tied to their unity in the kingdom.

We thus learn from Jesus that we are not called to ditch our families and replace them with the church. The point is that our sense of family changes as the kingdom community becomes central. The kingdom does not force us to abandon our biological families, even though the centrality of the kingdom in our lives may cause them to abandon us (1 Cor 7:15). Those who reject God's kingdom will certainly reject its prominent place in our lives. This is how the kingdom brings a sword to families (Matt 10:34–36). Those who believe that birth family comes first will feel threatened by the priority we give to church life. Jesus experienced this firsthand and he said that his followers would, too.

Loving and Hating our Family

This priority is what Jesus is talking about when he says that disciples must "hate" their family members (Luke 14:26). In English, the word "hate" is extremely strong. It carries tremendous emotional weight. Given the opportunity, many people would go out of their way to hurt someone they hated. We certainly don't use the word "hate" lightly. Like its counterpart, "love," we try to use it sparingly.

This is not how this language functions in Scripture. In much of Scripture, to "love" means to choose, while to "hate" means to leave unchosen. To love is to prioritize; to hate is not to prioritize. In this sense, God loved Jacob and hated Esau (Mal 1:2–3), and Jacob loved Rachel and hated Leah (Gen 29:30–33). Though God cared for and even prospered both men, only Jacob was chosen to carry forward God's promise to Abraham. Though Jacob provided for and fathered sons with both wives, Rachel was the wife he chose and therefore favored.

To love people is to direct more of our time, energy, and resources toward them. To hate people, in this sense, means to give comparatively less of our time, energy, and resources to them. Such hatred does not mean that someone is loathsome to us or that we shouldn't honor them. To feel hated is to feel left out while others are included. Jesus sometimes made his family feel that way. They felt that way because they lived in a world in which one's family got the lion's share of one's time, energy, and resources. Jesus' point was simple: in the kingdom, this prioritization changes, and that change can bring division.

Family in the Kingdom

There is no division, of course, when family members are equally committed to God's kingdom. They will accept with joy that we, too, have entered into new and abundant life. They won't feel threatened by our expanding family circle because theirs is also expanding. They will receive it as a gift that we have been grafted into God's massive family tree and will be nourished by the same deep roots.

In the Lord, our relationships with family members should improve. We will move beyond unhealthy dependence on only a few people, who may or may not be able to provide for all our needs. We will cease behaving according to rank and title and begin relating as brothers and sisters in Christ. We will not need to compete over the scarce resources and affection of our biological kin because we now share in the abundant and overflowing resources of God's kingdom community.

Most Christians already agree that the kingdom is like this. They believe that when Christ returns and brings his kingdom in its fullness that there will be a great social leveling. They anticipate that our sense of family will expand to include all believers everywhere. They look forward to quality relationships, without all the sinful division and competition that characterizes life in a fallen world. Not everyone seems to know, however, that the Bible invites us to experience this life now.

If the New Testament is right, this new humanity has already begun in Christ. We're already free from seeing people from a human point of view. This is good news! Many people live in terribly broken families. They've already experienced the limitations of biological families. Even if all their family relationships were now reconciled, it's not good news that their biological family is all they've got. They've tried the family-driven life and failed. It is good news that God has invited them to become a part of his family, *and* they don't have to wait until the afterlife to experience the love, joy, and companionship of God's kingdom.

The early church clearly viewed one another as family. They referred to one another as brothers and sisters. They used adoption language to describe what it meant to join God's family. They shared possessions and took care of one another's financial needs. They encouraged one another to share their blessings and their curses, their losses and their victories. As Paul put it, "If one member suffers, all suffer together with it; if one member is honored, all rejoice together with it" (1 Cor 12:26).

Embracing our life together as a church family is central to Christian witness. It's how the world will see that we love one another. It's how God chooses to draw all people to himself. We must therefore pursue it with great fervor. We must truly share our blessings and celebrate our accomplishments with fellow believers. We must share our losses by mourning together. We should find meaningful ways to celebrate holidays together and find creative ways to share life. What things are we doing separately that we might enjoy doing together? How might we creatively share possessions? Not every family needs to own expensive items that are used only once a year. Why not share a pressure washer, trailer, or sidewalk edger?

Living like family will require us to negotiate healthy boundaries and work through difficult conversations. This is what strong families must do. They don't give up or back away when trust is broken; they identify and work through problems. Conflict is not a sign of incompatibility, but a step toward true familial bonding. Family members will occasionally discipline one another gently for their own good, and so should church members.

Witness to Family

Living as a church family will also mean forming healthy ways of relating to biological family members who are not believers. Like Jesus, we must refuse to allow our biological families to call all the shots and control us.

We must send a clear message that God has adopted us into his household and that his kingdom is the centerpiece of our lives. At the same time, we must display and proclaim this news in a way that showcases its goodness. God's offer is for all people, including our unbelieving relatives. So we should honor them as parents, siblings, and children who are made in God's image and dearly beloved by him. We should seek their best interests and strive to live at peace with them.

We should also try to meet our family members' genuine needs to the best of our ability. But we cannot allow their every whim to monopolize our time, energy, and resources. Caring for them cannot be the organizing center of our lives because God's kingdom already is. We cannot serve two masters. This truth may incite resentment; it means that there are limits to what we are willing to do on behalf of family. Even so, we have good news to share with them: *we aren't the solution to their problems*. God's storehouse overflows with abundant treasures and he desires to pour them upon his children. We have begun to share in those treasures as part of God's family, and so can they.

Jesus found a way to remain in relationship with his unbelieving family members. Even though he did not make them the center of his universe, he remained close enough for them to see his life's central ambition. It took time, but after a while it seems that most of them made it their ambition as well. Jesus wasn't so close to them that God's kingdom couldn't be his center, but he wasn't so distant that they couldn't eventually see his center for the good news that it is. This sort of approach is reflected in Peter and Paul's advice to those who embraced God's kingdom before their spouses did: stay with them, but be a strong enough witness to win them over (1 Pet 3:1–2; 1 Cor 7:13–16).

Such talk about loving and hating, prioritizing some and not others may seem a bit over the top. Why draw such sharp lines? Why not just love everyone equally? Why not embrace the universal family of all God's creatures? A universal approach to love would certainly be more effective if the church's task were to attract as many people as possible to a better world to come. It would also be a great fit if our task were to make this world a better place.

Scripture just doesn't approach love and family this way. The church's primary mission is to cultivate a life together that is itself the better place into which God invites all people. The church is called to be the one space where self-giving love bubbles over in abundance regardless of birth family, social standing, and personal accomplishments. It is the kingdom of

God breaking into world history. People will never experience true love in our midst if kingdom citizens attempt to spend their affections equally upon all people everywhere or concentrate their time, energy, and resources on blood relatives or some other affinity group.

19

Friendship

THE LINE BETWEEN FAMILY and friends is a bit blurry. Usually, we identify our closest relationships *outside* of our biological family as "friendships." But that's not always the way it goes. Many people identify spouses, parents, or siblings as their best friends. They do so because they feel closer to them and spend more time with them than with anyone else.

We use the word *friend* to describe all kinds of relationships. We might become "friends" on Facebook with a high school classmate, even though we would never have called them friends when we were in school together. We use the same word to describe everyone from our best friends to our "study buddies."

In Jesus' day, one didn't use the word "friend" to describe acquaintances or people with whom you were merely friendly. Friendship, like love, meant a certain kind of relationship. Just as Jesus had a radical perspective on family, he also approached friendship in a unique way. His approach flows from the gospel—from the fact that God has called his people to be his better place in this world.

How Worldly Friendship Works

To fully appreciate Jesus' approach, it is helpful to compare it to a more common view of friendship. The following excerpt from HowStuffWorks.com captures popular thinking well:

> Friendship is a type of relationship between two people who care about each other. But such a dry definition doesn't do the

concept of friendship justice. Consider these examples: A friend is the first person you want to call when you hear good news. A friend remembers that you don't like pickles on your sandwich. A friend will accompany you on the most boring of errands and make them seem fun.

In other words, friendship is wonderful, and much ink has been spilled in citing the virtues of having friends. That's not to say friendship is easy, though. It demands time and effort, and it requires that people put someone other than themselves first sometimes. But in exchange for that work, a friend can provide an immense amount of support and comfort in good times and in bad.

Many qualities are necessary for a good friendship, including honesty, trustworthiness, loyalty and unconditional acceptance. A friendship should make both people in the relationship happy; both people should have fun when they spend time together. To be perfectly frank, that's a tall order. Human beings can clash very easily, which is why it's hard for some people to maintain many friendships. It's possible that friendship can exist between two people at one stage of life, but life changes and personal growth may make friendship impossible at another stage. It can be hard to meet the people who would make the perfect friend.[1]

At the end of the day, the most significant contribution that friends make, according to this article, is that they help us more deeply enjoy our lives. This article does a great job of summarizing how our culture views friendship, but it isn't Christian. It sounds self-serving, if nothing else—as if happiness and fun are the highest goals we can achieve. This resonates with many people's experience, whether believer or unbeliever. In fact, I suspect that most Christians in North America operate with this basic view of friendship. They do so at least in part because the church hasn't given them anything better to replace it with. Certainly, most churches warn against being self-centered. The danger comes when we fail to connect the dots between a self-centered world view and our notions of friendship. We don't hear about Christian friendship much and, if we do, the lessons reinforce what we've already absorbed from the world. Christians often assume that friendship is like water or bow ties; since we all know basically what they are, there is no need to examine them according to the Scriptures.

1. Edmonds, "What is Friendship?"

Jesus and Friendship

God's Word sheds fresh light on topics and practices that we think we already understand. It teaches us, for instance, that many "neutral" things matter, like how we dress, what we eat, who we date, and what we think about even when we have no intention of acting upon it. Friendship is one of those topics.

Consider what Jesus teaches about friendship in John 15:12–17:

> This is my commandment, that you love one another as I have loved you. No one has greater love than this, to lay down one's life for one's friends. You are my friends *if you do what I command you*. I do not call you servants any longer, because the servant does not know what the master is doing; but I have called you friends, *because I have made known to you everything that I have heard from my Father*. You did not choose me but I chose me. And I appointed you to go and bear fruit, fruit that will last, so that the Father will give you whatever you ask him in my name. I am giving you these commands so that you may love one another.

Jesus teaches us two important truths about friendship in this passage. First, friends love one another. Jesus defines that love radically: the greatest act of love is to lay down one's life for one's friend. This is a key difference between shallow relationships and true friendship. Christians are not selfish with their friends. They are self-giving, even to the point of death.

Second, Christian friendship is rooted in being about the same thing, and we can't be about the same thing unless we fully disclose ourselves to one another. In verse 15, Jesus says, "I do not call you servants any longer, because the servant does not know what the master is doing; but I have called you friends, because I have made known to you everything that I have heard from my Father." Jesus' disciples are transformed from servants into friends when he tells them everything he knows about God's kingdom and when they are willing to abide in those teachings as he does—to do what he commands. When they get on the same page as Jesus, in thought and deed, the disciples become partners with him in kingdom work. Jesus' friends are those who are as obsessed with the kingdom as he is.

Jesus' friends were not an ordinary group of folks. They were not the type of people who were likely to grab a cup of coffee together or text funny comments back and forth. Jesus' disciples included tax collectors and Zealots. Most people despised tax collectors, but Zealots despised them the most. Zealots sought to overthrow the corrupt Roman government, even staging violent demonstrations against it. Tax collectors served as the financial backbone of that government. They may have even been targeted by Zealots. Only Jesus could take such a potentially explosive group and make them friends.

Here's the point: in the kingdom, friendship isn't rooted in shared hobbies, taste in movies, sense of humor, or even good chemistry; it is rooted in a common commitment to God's reign. Since that reign is all-encompassing, those who are obsessed with it find themselves caring about the same things, living by the same principles, and valuing the same goods.

Many Christians throughout history have suggested similar ideas. Saint Augustine approached friendship this way, as did the medieval Cistercian monk Aelred of Rievaulx. Aelred identifies three kinds of friendship: (1) *carnal friendship*, which originates from and revolves around mutual love for immorality; (2) *worldly friendship*, which originates from and revolves around personal advantage and worldly ambition; and (3) *spiritual friendship*, which is life together in Christ.[2] In all three kinds, what constitutes friendship is the fact that the persons involved are about the same thing, they are on a common journey.

As believers we become people with tremendous potential for friendship with one another. My own life illustrates this quite clearly. In high school, I was friends with anyone who wanted the same things I did: partying on weekends, chasing girls, and listening to music that my parents despised. When I became a believer, I stopped enjoying those things. I started choosing my activities differently and seeking different things in life. So my friends and I eventually grew apart. The problem was not that I was more mature in the faith than they were, but that they didn't have faith and I did. My priorities changed, and theirs didn't.

Eventually I bumped into a guy named Brad, who was a believer my age. We quickly became best friends. Though we were from different school districts, played different sports, and had different interests, our faith drew us together. A few years later, I enrolled at Great Lakes Christian College and found an abundance of friends. At this point I also began to develop healthy friendships with people who were very different

---

2. Dutton, ed., *Aelred of Rievaulx*.

from me. Looking back, I realize that this was when I learned how to truly respect and befriend females. I also started cultivating friendships with people who were decades older than me.

Differences that formerly divided us just didn't matter anymore. It didn't matter that we listened to different music, wore different clothes, and rooted for different sports teams. It didn't matter that we were different genders, hailed from different states or countries, and were of different ages and generations. We followed the same Lord according to the same Scriptures and, to the extent that we followed him with our entire lives, we found ourselves becoming better and better friends with one another.

Friendship with the World

Can there be genuine friendship between those who follow Jesus and those who do not? The Apostle Paul gives an answer in 2 Corinthians 6:14–18:

> Do not be mismatched with unbelievers. For what partnership is there between righteousness and lawlessness? Or what fellowship is there between light and darkness? What agreement does Christ have with Beliar? Or what does a believer share with an unbeliever? What agreement has the temple of God with idols? For we are the temple of the living God; as God said, "I will live in them and walk among them, and I will be their God, and they shall be my people. Therefore come out from them, and be separate from them, says the Lord, and touch nothing unclean; then I will welcome you, and I will be your father, and you shall be my sons and daughters, says the Lord Almighty."

This is a tough passage to hear. It's so stark. Paul just says, "No."

Usually, if we quote this passage at all, we do so in the context of marriage between believers and unbelievers. Although this passage certainly applies to marriage, it applies more broadly than that.

Before I go any further, let me be clear that this cannot mean shunning unbelievers. Jesus took time for sinners and tax collectors, albeit Jewish ones. He ate and drank with them. He spent enough time with them that outsiders called them his friends (Matt 11:18–19). Jesus cultivated genuine relationships with those who weren't yet believers.

It is important to note, however, that Jesus himself never called unbelievers his friends. He only identified as friends those who embraced his kingdom legacy. He honored all people—even his enemies—and he made time for them. But Jesus didn't call them his friends. He made clear to everyone, including his family, that kingdom-seeking people came first.

At baptism, believers commit to seeking first God's kingdom with their whole life. This is why Christians shouldn't marry unbelievers and why Paul says that Christians aren't married like the world is married (1 Cor 7:29). To bind oneself to someone who does not put the kingdom first is to abandon the kingdom as one's primary commitment. Christians should only marry because they believe they can best seek first God's kingdom as someone who is wed to this other kingdom seeker.

We don't marry to bring meaning to our life; Jesus is our meaning. We don't marry to secure our finances; Jesus is our security. We don't marry so we can finally have a family; Jesus gives us a family. We marry only believers because only a believer can be as obsessed with the kingdom as we are.

But that's marriage—a much more formal relationship than friendship. How does this teaching apply to our friends?

Jason is a good friend of mine. He and I discussed this topic not too long ago. During that discussion, Jason expressed an objection based on his experience. He and an unbeliever from work are very close friends, he said. They love spending time together. They laugh a lot and quote lines from the same movies. They know each other well and contact each other whenever they have exciting news to share. In short, their relationship embodies all the great things identified by HowStuffWorks.com.

Jason is clued in to something. There can be genuine affinity between believers and unbelievers. But the Bible doesn't call that friendship. It doesn't really have a word for this kind of relationship. Because it is based on good chemistry—on "liking" one another—I am tempted to call it "likemanship." When you like being around someone because they make you laugh and cause you to lose track of time, you are falling "in like" with them.

The kind of friendship Jesus cultivated goes beyond "liking" in the way that love goes beyond infatuation. We know what infatuation looks like: teenagers admiring peers or celebrities from a distance. They don't really get to know them intimately, but they are attracted to them. They like their personality, and they can imagine building the rest of their lives around that person. They may tape posters of their "crush" all over their walls and scribble "I love so-and-so" all over their notebooks. They might even obsessively stalk their crush's Facebook page.

But that's not love. We might call it "puppy love" and find it cute. We don't take it seriously because we know it's not love. We don't get too worried about it because we know it's actually just infatuation. In a similar way, much of what passes for friendship is just "liking." When Christ calls us his friends, he means something far deeper, far more costly, and far more compelling than this kind of mutual attraction.

Surely, we suppose, Christians can witness best by developing and modeling the deeper kind of friendship to which Jesus calls us—especially with unbelievers. At this point, the Apostle Paul stops us right in our tracks: "What fellowship is there between light and darkness? What agreement does Christ have with Beliar? Or what does a believer share with an unbeliever?" (2 Cor 6:14–15). How can we truly be friends with those who don't believe?

Scripture presents friendship as companionship on a shared journey, not enjoyment of shared time. Believers and unbelievers are not on the same journey, even though they may have a lot in common and may develop a strong sense of fondness for one another. They can have good chemistry, and that chemistry may deepen into something more. They can appreciate one another's humor. They can share the kinds of common interests that make for endless small talk and interesting conversations. They might like to hang out and draw energy from one another. But they're not friends in Jesus' sense. They can't be. They can never truly be friends until either the believer stops obsessing about the kingdom or the unbeliever embraces that obsession, like Jesus' disciples did.

"Likemanship" has great value. It means more than the infatuation analogy may imply. Many Christians build incredibly enjoyable relationships with believers and unbelievers among their family, co-workers, and neighbors. It's fun to share a lot in common with another person and to enjoy each other's company. It's possible that we might enjoy spending time with a nonbeliever more than with some members of our church family.

Such relationships aren't bad and need not be avoided. They are one of the precious gifts God gives us to enjoy. They are also central to Christian mission. Jesus built this kind of relationship with sinners and tax collectors. He created space in his life to overlap with their lives so he might show and share the kingdom with them. Christians should actively pursue these sorts of relationships. Evangelism requires it.

But if we wish to keep with the biblical definition, we wouldn't call that friendship. We wouldn't cheapen the term lest believers lose sight of the unique bond we share because of Christ—the unique relationship we share with one another in God's kingdom.

Even if they take a while to discover, there are boundaries between a believer and an unbeliever that one or both of them won't be able to cross. Such relationships can only deepen so far. For them to move beyond "likemanship" to friendship requires one or both persons to rearrange their priorities.

Friendship evangelism· is dangerous in the same way that missionary dating is dangerous. Those who seek *first* God's kingdom can only prioritize unbelievers at the expense of the kingdom community. Otherwise, their love will be divided. The unique love between believers will not stand out and draw people to God because their love isn't unique after all; it's what believers can have with anyone whose company they enjoy enough.

Friendship entails knowing and being on board with the same things as another person. That's a hard truth. But it's a biblical truth. When we disregard this truth, we misrepresent ourselves to the nonbelievers with whom we want to be friends in the truest sense of the word. The world already has enough of that kind of falsehood. The world already knows that kind of relationship. Let's model something better.

This doesn't mean that believers should go around unfriending people. It doesn't mean we should dissolve quality relationships with unbelieving co-workers, neighbors, and spouses. It didn't mean that for the Apostle Paul, who encouraged believers to remain married to their unbelieving spouses (1 Cor 7:12–16). Nor does it mean that we have to go around correcting people when they call someone "friend" who is not really on the same life's journey as them. Jesus did not teach us about true friendship in order to deputize us as his word police.

This is partly the case because the term *friendship* may be used metaphorically. If we have a co-worker with whom we watch Marvel movies religiously, we might call them our "Marvel friend." They are our companions on the Marvel movie journey. If they don't seek first the kingdom, though, they cannot be our life's journey companion. They might be our hobby companion, our book club friend, or even our work friend. Again, there is nothing wrong with such limited unions. I am not drawing attention to the core substance of friendship in order to depreciate our relationships with unbelievers, but to fully appreciate the precious value of the friends we have in Christ.

True Friends

It should go without saying that nonbelievers may also become friends with one another. They can be on the same page as one another, and their friendship can possess great power. God recognizes such power in the Babel account of Genesis 11. All the people of the earth were of one mind, spoke one language, and possessed one agenda. God knew that with such friendship they could do anything they set their minds to. Unfortunately, they set their minds to disobeying God's command to be fruitful, multiply, and fill the earth. They sought, instead, to make a name for themselves by building an impressive city. In befriending one another in this way, they became enemies of God. As Jesus' brother says in James 4:4, "Do you not know that friendship with the world is enmity with God? Therefore whoever wishes to be a friend of the world becomes an enemy of God."

Christians are those whose common friendship with God makes them friends with one another. It is blatantly false to claim—and I've heard this countless times—that certain members of the body of Christ cannot be friends because they "don't have anything in common." They both have the kingdom! How can they have nothing in common? If any two members of Christ's body cannot find a friend in each other, it is because one or both of them is not seeking first God's kingdom.

In John 3:16 we are told that God loved the world so much that he sent Jesus. God sent Jesus so everyone who believes may have eternal life. Jesus then tells believers to love one another so the world may come to believe. John does not say that because God loved the world we should, too. Unlike God, we lack the ability to rain or shine on all people at the same time. Human finitude means that we must prioritize our time, energy, and resources. John makes it abundantly clear where our priorities must lie and who our true friends really are.

True friendship is costly. It risks making tough choices. It risks being misunderstood. It risks alienating people. If the church's primary responsibility were to prepare people *for* a better place somewhere else, then such risks don't quite seem worth it. Friendship with the world would be a powerful tool for attracting people to Jesus. In fact, if our goal were to prepare as many people as possible for a better place somewhere else, then it would be best to spend less time cultivating friendships with those who are already prepared and more time cultivating friendships with those who are not. We'll have all of eternity to spend with the saved. Time on earth is short, so we should invest as much of it as possible in those who are lost. This logic is sound, but it's not what we find in Scripture.

Friendship with the world would also be a powerful tool for making the world a better place. There are plenty of good-natured and resourceful unbelievers whose lives revolves around improving society and caring for those less fortunate. If fixing this world were the church's responsibility, then it would be highly advantageous to make friends with people in high places. They would grant us easy access to the most efficient and powerful tools of social change.

Yet Jesus never went this way and his brother James strictly forbade it (Jas 2 and 4). They resisted strategic alliances with influential nonbelievers because they represent a different world. Those best positioned to make this world a better place are in the worst position to embrace God's better place as a gift. They have to lose influence in this world in order to embrace God's better world. This is part of what Jesus meant when he said that the first will be last and the last first. It's why the rich find it nearly impossible to enter the kingdom (Mark 10:25).

Jesus' radical approach to friendship makes the most sense if it is the church's responsibility to be the better place that God has already begun to make in this world. And this notion of the church's responsibility makes the most sense only if it is God's all-wise strategy for drawing all people to himself.

INTERLUDE

God's Kingdom and Social Justice

ONE OF THE TASKS of this book has been to demonstrate how it could be that God's people are not responsible for *making* this world a better place, but for *being* the better place that Christ has already made and that the wider world won't be until Christ returns. It should be clear by now that this doesn't mean that Christians should stick to saving souls and leave social activism to everyone else. The gospel is inherently social. It brings forth a church that lives out God's vision for humanity and showcases God's justice before the watching world.

God has not, however, called the church to demand justice from this world. We are not God's instrument for making the world a better place. God has created us to be the living picture, the pilot project, the first fruits of his kingdom and his justice. This was entirely God's doing. We receive our new identity as a gift that we did nothing to deserve.

God has entrusted his kingdom to us, but this is not a mandate to force it upon those who reject the kingdom. It is a divine initiative, accomplishment, and gift all the way down. It is a gift for us and it must be a gift for any who receive it through us. Our job is to embrace that gift, display it, and proclaim its availability to others.

The idea of "*just* embracing God's gift" sounds like quietism—the misguided notion that churches should live in a holy bubble, keep their hands clean, and never truly enter the fray of this world's brokenness. This is simply not the case. God has sent us into a broken world to make visible his kingdom and to proclaim its implications for all of creation. The early church got into trouble with the public authorities precisely because they refused to hide under a bushel and keep their mouths shut.

Yet we shouldn't assume that early Christian proclamation took the same form it takes among the religious Right and Left of our day. The early believers didn't go around reprimanding people for not living by kingdom principles that they never agreed to follow. Nor did they infiltrate elite circles of social influence in order to manipulate laws and customs for the good of the masses. Instead, they were *vocal* in proclaiming the gospel of God's kingdom and *visible* in living it out as a community. They passed it along just like the gift they received it to be.

We can focus on bearing good news in these ways because God uses other institutions to keep wickedness in check. He uses the powers and principalities to make this world as good as it can be while the majority of humans remain in a state of rebellion against their creator. Since God *has not* called the church to make this world a better place and *has* called other entities to do so, does this mean Christians may play no part in improving this world?

Again, it does not. Christians may, indeed, contribute to world improvement without forsaking our fundamental calling. We may even do so as a part of fulfilling that calling. I explore some of these ways in the remaining chapters, beginning with our place in the workforce.

20

Vocation

THE TERM *VOCATION* REFERS to a person's life calling. Most people equate it with their occupation or nine-to-five job, but it doesn't have to involve money or some other form of compensation. In fact, raising a family or devoting one's time, energy, and passions to a specific cause might also be considered one's vocation. The concept of vocation has a long history in the church. This history is worth reviewing because it provides valuable information for understanding how Christians might best serve as witnesses at work.[1]

For Jesus and the disciples, seeking first God's kingdom was the believer's all-encompassing vocation. Fixing or running the world was outside of their purview. They trusted God to use others to take care of that. For a few centuries, Christians were content to leave it that way. But then the Roman Empire made Christianity the imperial religion. After that, all governmental functions became positions that Christians had to occupy, by default. There were quite simply no other candidates. To be a Roman meant being a Christian.

This posed a new challenge to the church. Jesus' teachings about the kingdom were terribly impractical for running the Roman Empire. An imperial powerhouse cannot continue to dominate by following Jesus' commandments. Rulers can't keep criminals off the streets and barbarians outside their borders by turning their cheeks and washing their enemies' feet. A governor cannot increase the power of the emperor's household by giving his possessions to the poor and forgiving debtors.

---

1. For more of this history, see Nugent, "Kingdom Work."

Thus many Christians who took up these roles began to think about their jobs through the lens of natural law. Rather than looking to Jesus, they tried to heed the principles of cause and effect that the creator had built into his creation. This meant learning the lessons that God teaches through nature, history, and experience. We can still learn much from God, they affirmed, without following the teachings of Jesus.

What purpose, then, could Jesus' kingdom vision possibly serve? His teachings couldn't be ignored altogether. Though they weren't useful in governing the Roman world, many Christians believed that the kingdom to come would still be guided by them. That being the case, Jesus' vision must be preserved. Kingdom-minded individuals must somehow keep it alive.

This is why medieval convents and monasteries were so significant. Devout men and women took vows of poverty and chastity and committed to the special calling of perpetuating the kingdom vision of Jesus. All sorts of occupations were necessary to keep the world running smoothly, but monks and nuns stood out for their unique service to God and humanity. For many centuries, the Holy Roman Empire viewed these believers as having a special calling or vocation from God. Everyone else just had ordinary jobs.

The great Reformer, Martin Luther, took exception to the notion that only a select group of Christians were uniquely called by God. He sought to give dignity to each person's calling. To collect taxes, uphold public order, and contribute to the local economy is, in his view, to love one's neighbor and fulfill one's calling from God. But one does not carry out such tasks according to the way of Jesus. So Luther instructed believers to obey natural law in the public sphere and Jesus' teaching in their private life and church life.

Since the Reformation, it has become increasingly common for Christians to identify their work in the public sphere as their vocation. It has also been common to maintain Luther's firm distinction between public and private life. Religion was relegated to the private sphere, of course. Though it has taken various forms, natural law continues to guide workforce ethics, whereas kingdom principles are often limited to home and church life.

Vocation and a Better Place

Our view of a better place deeply impacts our approach to vocation. In the heaven-centered view, the Christian's primary vocation is to prepare people for the better place to come. The workplace, then, is the ideal place to meet and build relationships with those who are not yet prepared for heaven. The main goal is to lead them into a saving relationship with Jesus. Time spent at work is also valuable because it helps believers pay the bills and support the church's mission.

In the world-centered view, vocation is linked directly to "kingdom" work. Since God's people are tasked with making this world better, work sites are prime places for doing this. If our jobs involve healing the sick, feeding the hungry, and caring for prisoners, then we are already fulfilling our kingdom mandate forty hours a week. Given that Christians spend so much more time at work than in church, congregations should emphasize equipping their members with what they need to fulfill their kingdom vocation in the workplace. Church gatherings participate in kingdom work mostly by preparing people for what they will do outside of the assembly. That's where most service to the world happens. Though it couldn't happen without the support of the church, kingdom work takes place mostly outside of it.

The kingdom-centered approach is quite different. If the church's primary vocation is to be the better place God has made through Christ, then most of this work can only take place in the common life of the church. We proclaim the good news beyond the assembly of believers, but we can't forget the substance of that proclamation: *the kingdom isn't work believers do but a work that God has done on our behalf. It is a gift that God has given us to embrace and display in our love-filled life together.*

For individual believers this often means that our *occupations*—in and of themselves—cannot be our primary *vocation*, whatever good it may be doing for the world. Seeking first God's kingdom remains primary. Yet we cannot serve two masters, so the jobs that pay our bills should play an integral part in our overriding kingdom vocation.

This does not mean that everyone must work for the church. It means that our time at work, like our time at home and with the church, is a time for embracing, displaying, and proclaiming God's kingdom. It should be clear to fellow employees that our job is not the most important thing in our life. They should know by our speech and actions that we believe we have been born anew into an abundant life of love in God's kingdom and that we experience new life first and foremost among God's people.

Our relationship to our professions should be much like our relationship to our biological families. They are a part of who we are, they are important, and we honor them. But they must not become the organizing center of our lives. Our relationship to our jobs may also be compared to "likemanship." We may really enjoy what we are doing and time might fly by while we're doing it, but we can only be friends of Jesus by making his life's passion our life's passion—and we have only enough energy for one life's passion.

Though God does not hold the church responsible for making the world better, certain occupations provide believers with valuable opportunities to meet real needs, protect God's good creation, and genuinely improve the lives of many people. The Apostle Paul found tent-making to be a viable and strategic trade. There is no reason to disdain jobs that entail caring for the needy, conserving our natural resources, or settling conflicts between hostile parties.

There are countless ways to contribute to the common good and to make a positive difference in people's lives. There are endless opportunities for making this world a bit better. However, it must be remembered that even if a particular job seizes such an opportunity, it is not therefore "kingdom" work. It is not of the kingdom if it does not participate in the Spirit's work of *forming* communities that embrace, display, and proclaim God kingdom, and *scattering* them throughout the world as witnesses to God's accomplished work through Christ. It may be good work and well worth our time, but it's not our vocation.

Kingdom Witness at Work

Though good work and kingdom witness are not the same, believers may still bear witness to God's kingdom through their jobs. Indeed, since our whole life exists to seek first God's kingdom, we need to connect our work to the church's life together. But how?

One way is to pursue paid employment together as a kingdom community. In other words, if we meet a particular need together through some sort of shared trade (like daycare), the nature of our togetherness can itself point to God's kingdom. The way we love each other and serve alongside each other can express the new humanity God has made of us.

The way we view one another from beyond a human point of view, the way that the first among us is last and the last first, the way that leaders serve and every person's contributions are equally valued—any and all of these realities powerfully displays God's kingdom through the specific work we are doing. This work's connection to the kingdom is not that it makes the world better but that it embraces, displays, and proclaims God's better world.

It is more challenging, but it is not impossible, to point to the kingdom through forms of employment beyond the kingdom community. We can still do our work in such a way that God's kingdom is displayed and others can see that we are part of something much bigger than ourselves and our jobs. To the extent that our employment allows, we can perform our work in light of kingdom principles that we learned as functioning members of the kingdom community.

Christ has taught us what the kingdom is like, we have experienced that likeness firsthand as a part of his body, and we can apply that experience in our jobs. We do so because Christ's lordship over all things means that his way is right in all things. No matter our occupation, our vocation remains the same. Thus, while working in our chosen occupations, we may display God's kingdom.

We display kingdom economics in how we manage business finances. When relating to offenders at work, we display kingdom justice. We show kingdom hospitality in how we welcome whatever children and social misfits we encounter. Without being asked or told, we perform our work according to the way of Jesus. In doing so, we display his kingdom in our job performance—if only in a fragmentary way. And when others see the purity and reverence of our lives and ask us to give an account for our strange work, we boldly proclaim God's kingdom and testify to the life-transforming impact of the kingdom community.

No matter what our occupation may be, there are almost always three basic ways to bear witness to God's kingdom. The first has to do with how we carry out our assigned responsibilities. Will we be faithful and content with the work we have been given to do or will we covet authority that hasn't been given to us and resent those to whom it has been given? In a world where first is first and last is last, we can display our newfound security in Christ by not constantly craving that which is not ours for the taking.

We may also bear witness to God's kingdom by treating fellow employees equally. In the world, people give special treatment to others based on their accomplishments (education, longevity, status), how attractive they are (likability, compatibility, appearance), accidents of birth (sex, age, ethnicity), and acquisitions of choice (faith, possessions, morals). As a part of the body of Christ, we have learned to treat all people equally. Our uncommon ability to do so at work should stand out as a powerful testimony to God's kingdom.

A third way to bear witness to God's kingdom at work has to do with our exercise of power. We follow 1 Peter's advice and submit to our superiors even when they don't deserve it. This is not about buttering them up in hopes of benefiting later on. Rather, it is about honoring all people and showing them a better way. If we find ourselves in positions of authority, we heed Jesus' instruction to serve those who are beneath us and not lord over them. People are accustomed to being bullied or run over by those above them. Managers who truly seek the best interests of those they manage and truly value the insights and abilities of those "beneath" them will truly stand out in displaying a better way.

We may also gain the respect of peers who work on the same level as us. We may do so quite simply by choosing not to compete with them. In God's kingdom there is always enough to go around. So if we receive a little less at work, our needs will by no means go unmet. All things are already ours in Christ (1 Cor 3:21–23), so we need not alienate others by increasing our share at their expense. This truth enables us to display and proclaim the peace of Christ in ways that are sure to pique the interests of our peers.

As long as our job gives us tasks to do and people to work with, the wisdom of God's kingdom will provide a better way for us to conduct ourselves. We can be noticeably mature in our contentment, impartiality, and security. Our life in Christ's body makes this second nature to us. If we truly live this way, people will notice and ask. When they do, we will be prepared to proclaim the goodness of God's kingdom and the abundance of love we experience among God's people.

Choosing Jobs for the Kingdom

Some Christians have few choices when it comes to employment. Their abilities, opportunities, and economic needs demand that they pursue a particular line of work. Yet those who have the luxury of choosing their employment shouldn't squander it. Since believers seek first God's kingdom even in our jobs, we should choose those jobs as strategically as possible. There are a number of questions we might ask to help us determine what sort of job to pursue.

- What jobs best enable us to display and proclaim God's kingdom?

- What jobs situate us in places that desperately need churches to embrace, display, and proclaim God's kingdom?

- What jobs won't monopolize our time, passions, and energy?

- What jobs are compatible with our witness to God's kingdom?

- What jobs shape us to be the kind of people the kingdom is shaping us to be?

- What jobs help us meet specific needs within Christ's body?

- What jobs give our church access to resources that will strengthen our witness?

In choosing our occupations, we should avoid jobs that monopolize our time, shape us to be unlike the kingdom, and harm the body of Christ. Yet, a spirit of creativity and stewardship should dictate the Christian's choice of vocation, not predetermined legalistic prohibitions. We should not ask, "What am I allowed or not allowed to do?" but "What contributes positively to our church's witness to God's kingdom?"

21

Missions

IT'S NOT TOO HARD to figure out what mission work looks like in the various approaches to a better place that we have considered. If God's people are called to prepare others for a better place somewhere else (heaven centered), then missions revolves around finding lost people and convincing them that they need Jesus. It may also involve helping converts sustain life changes, but only enough to remain in God's good graces until they die. If God's people are called to make this world a better place (world centered), missions revolves around identifying places of need, creating institutions best suited for meeting those needs, and sustaining those institutions. As Christians, missionaries perform this service in the name of Jesus and are thus happy to teach the people they help about Jesus and lead them into a right relationship with him. Yet, a kingdom-centered approach will have different priorities.

Kingdom-Centered Mission

The church's calling centers on *being* the better place God began in Jesus. Kingdom-centered mission therefore identifies places that need a vibrant witness to God's kingdom and establishes and sustains churches to be that witness. No matter what broader needs exist in those places, the church's mission remains the same. Still, it is difficult to witness the effects of gospel ignorance—social injustice, economic scarcity, and educational deprivation—without feeling immense, heartfelt compassion and even indignation. We can and should feel those things. But our response, the response to which God calls us, remains the same: to fill the earth with churches that embrace, display, and proclaim his kingdom in dark places. What a wonderful gift God has given us!

Planting kingdom-centered churches will bring God's people into meaningful contact with the brokenness of the communities where we live. So it makes a lot of sense to stack fledgling churches with founding members who have the right skills to engage the community's needs. If impure water is a major problem, then it would be ideal to send water purification specialists as part of the church-planting team.

Even so, the new church's priority has to be displaying and proclaiming God's kingdom. In their occupations, all church members should seek the well-being of the cities where they live (Jer 29:7). Their presence in the workforce is salt, light, and leaven. They work in such a way that co-workers and those whom they serve can see the wisdom of God's kingdom in the disciple's performance. This, in turn, opens the door for disciples to proclaim God's kingdom and invite others to experience the faith community that sustains them.

Some approaches to mission have this shortcoming: their gospel message or approach to meeting social needs is divorced from God's strategy of local church witness. They fail to proclaim the new world in the midst of the old. This is not to say it is wrong for Christians to work with nonprofit or parachurch organizations. Sometimes the best way to meet a particular need or reach a particular people group is through a structure quite different from a local church body. But this does not justify demoting or abandoning God's strategy as set forth in Scripture. Parachurch structures that wish to align with God's mission must be rooted in and tilted toward local churches. If they want to move beyond good work to kingdom witness, the local church must be integral to the service they render.

By "integral" I do not mean that they rely upon churches merely to pay their bills and provide eager workers. Christ did not found the church in order to staff and underwrite parachurch organizations. I mean that these organizations see the local church as central to God's mission. Their role is to point others to the new humanity and new creation that is visible on earth only in the church. They have not finished their task until they have incorporated the disciples they make into a local church family.

It is important to get this relationship right. The church does not support parachurch ministries which, in turn, do the kingdom work.

Rather, parachurch ministries serve people and then direct them to the church, which incorporates them into God's kingdom work.

NO: Church → Parachurch → God's kingdom

YES: Parachurch → Church → God's kingdom

All too often, those who are passionate about reaching a particular people group or addressing a specific social injustice see themselves as the ones doing kingdom work and the church as their wealthy patron. They therefore invite churches to be active in kingdom work by partnering with their particular organization, which is portrayed as being on the front line or in the trenches of real mission.

This approach recasts the church into the role of a booster club, a support group. The church functions as a volunteer club that raises funds, plans events, and rallies people around their "team." To be sure, many teams would not be able to play were it not for their booster club and all the fans the club recruits to support them. These fans identify with their team, but they seldom step foot on the playing field. When they do, it is only to greet the players, admire their work, and maybe fantasize about being part of the actual game.

And so it is with many mission organizations. The missionary—whether a campus minister, poverty relief worker, or evangelist to an unreached people group—will visit local churches to explain the great needs they see and are uniquely poised to meet. They then ask these churches to do whatever they can to raise funds to support this work. The church is welcome to visit the mission field and see this work in action, but seldom are they expected to stay and join the work full time.

It may be the case that many Christians in North America would rather remain in their pews where their own needs are met. In this situation, missionaries can serve as living links between congregations and the actual mission field. Through Facebook, email, presentations, and a few short-term visits, churchgoers can experience the mission secondhand. A few exceptionally active individuals do the kingdom work, and the mostly sedentary masses support the cause and foot the bill from the sidelines. *But*, Christianity isn't a spectator sport!

New Testament missionaries certainly did not relate to the church in this way. The churches in Acts were the product of mission. Motivated by persecution and empowered by the Spirit, new Christians went forth from Jerusalem spreading the gospel and establishing churches that were committed to embracing, displaying, and proclaiming the kingdom.

One such church was established in Antioch (Acts 11). Barnabas sent for Paul, and together they strengthened this congregation for over a year, bringing many people into the church family. That church, in turn, gave generously in order to support Christians in Judea who were struggling financially. Eventually, they discerned by God's Spirit that they should send Paul and Barnabas abroad to plant and strengthen other churches further west (Acts 13).

This is God's design: churches committed to God's kingdom strengthen other churches committed to God's kingdom and continue planting still more churches committed to God's kingdom. All of them are involved in the same work. But congregations carry out this work in different ways according to the specific needs and resources of their particular places.

Every church is the site of God's kingdom work, and every church should be concerned that more sites are established throughout the world. No congregation is supposed to be more active in kingdom work than another. Each one *is* God's kingdom work. There are no spectators. To be the body of Christ is to be a firsthand participant in God's work. It is to be the new humanity and display God's new creation.

Church and Social Needs

God's people can minister to specific people groups and meet specific needs in a variety of ways. We've already discussed one of those ways: through our occupations, whether we work for the powers or for parachurch organizations. In addition, church members can work together to reach specific people and meet specific needs. That work can be part of their common life together. How they carry out that work would be an extension of their corporate witness to God's kingdom. Together they pray and study God's word, together they meet the needs of the entire body, and together they serve their community in various ways.

Take, for example, the witness of Englewood Christian Church in Indianapolis, Indiana. Situated in an economically depressed neighborhood, they have committed to living a robust life together that reflects God's kingdom. In the past, core members had left the neighborhood and relocated to the suburbs. In recent years, they began returning. Many members moved next door to one another and became lovingly present to each other throughout the week. They embraced kingdom living as God's gift and displayed it publicly to all their neighbors.

It wasn't long before they found creative ways to make their new life more visible and accessible to those neighbors. Together they formed a community development corporation that took possession of abandoned houses, remodeled them to be habitable, and made them available for reasonable prices—first to church members and then to unbelievers. This work, which meets a specific social need in a way that reflects God's justice, is part of the church's life together. It is *their* work. Together they also started offering childcare, accounting services, and a bookstore to serve one another as well as their unbelieving neighbors.

Some members travel into the city to work in a variety of jobs. Others gather with fellow believers on or near church property to carry out the work of community development, childcare, and their other businesses. The kingdom principles that govern their worship life also inform their work life and home life. They refuse to divorce church life and social action. Their life together *is* social action.

So there are at least three ways that believers might participate in meeting this world's needs and making a positive difference in their cities without compromising or eclipsing the church's primary calling to be the better place God began in Jesus:

- Believers may get a job in a particular field that is run by the powers and principalities and make a living from that work, all the while seeking first God's kingdom in the local church as the organizing center and ultimate passion of their lives.

- Believers may form parachurch organizations that are dedicated to meeting particular needs and are committed to the integral involvement of local churches. They will funnel the people they serve into those churches and not treat them like booster clubs. One sign of healthy integration is that members of such organization see their local church life as their most fundamental participation in God's kingdom work and not subservient to their parachurch work.

- As part of the church's life together, believers may take on a particular cause and champion that cause together as a church family. Their congregation will be the organization that helps out and it will do so in ways that embrace, display, and proclaim God's kingdom above all else. Where churches are not already present, they will plant one. They will be certain to form it around a nucleus of kingdom-minded people so God may draw people to himself through their love for one another.

When Disaster Strikes

Another popular form of mission work involves disaster relief. Christians routinely flock to areas that have experienced hurricanes, tornados, floods, or tsunamis. But we are not the only ones doing so. There's no shortage of humanitarians and philanthropists poised to jump from one needy cause to another. Should the church seek to join them when disaster strikes? Is it our job to duplicate the work of worldly benefactors, albeit in Jesus' name? Can we do basically the same thing, as long as we also invite people to follow Jesus? Or should churches do nothing at all and just leave it to the powers and do-gooders?

If there is a demand for a specific skill set, church members may find themselves being called upon to work in a particular area as a simple extension of their paying jobs. It's not necessarily kingdom witness, but it honors all people and gives an opportunity to use kingdom principles acquired at church to offer creative solutions that unbelievers may lack the vision to see. Skilled believers should not compromise their witness or scandalize unbelievers by sitting on the sidelines. They should be there when everyone else in their field is there, but they should be there, unlike everyone else, *as Christians*. That service—while not the church's mission or God's kingdom work—is still good work.

Churches in the immediate vicinity of a disaster should be especially eager to serve by using their abilities and resources to help their towns in times of need. Christian love and kingdom witness demand that they prioritize the needs of the body, but churches typically have more than enough resources to do that. Their overflow should spill onto others in ways that bring unbelievers into contact with God's kingdom. For this to happen, the body must serve together as a group, not separately as heroic individuals. The helping hand we lend is not itself kingdom work, but the witness of the body serving together should boldly display God's kingdom.

It is also quite possible that new churches are needed to provide able bodies to help out and assimilate new people. Hurting people don't need just a helping hand and they don't need just Jesus. They need to be incorporated into a new humanity that will help them reorder their lives in accordance with God's gift to them. They need to be part of a kingdom-embracing church.

Most philanthropists and benefactors will help out until they run out of resources or vacation time. Then they return to their comfortable lives. Churches, on the other hand, will remain steadfast for years, even decades, as gradual, sometimes imperceptible growth takes place and communities begin to piece together their post-disaster lives.

Most philanthropists and benefactors will enter the victim's turf for a while in order to lend a helping hand, but they will seldom welcome such people into their homes. Disaster-stricken areas will therefore need homes and communities in which disaster victims may take refuge. As they begin to rebuild their lives, they will be right where they need to be to hear the good news. God invites them for the long haul into a community of abundance in which there are more brothers, sisters, aunts, and uncles than they've ever had.

The church's role is crucial. It's just not a Christianized version of the roles that others play. We don't come just bringing help; we come proclaiming good news of the newness that God has already accomplished on behalf of this world. We come offering not just hope for the afterlife, but the experience of new life now on a firm foundation that will never be wiped out by floods, storms, quakes, and wars.

22

Witness to the Powers

IF WE'VE ESTABLISHED ANYTHING so far, it's that improving the world is secondary to the church's true calling. We have provided a detailed articulation of our primary call and discussed a few ways Christians may help improve the world. But this discussion would be incomplete without addressing our witness to the powers. In chapter 6, I introduced the powers as governing institutions that God uses to maintain order in society by keeping evil under control and promoting the well-being of those in their charge. The powers most talked about in Scripture include angels, governors, religious authorities, masters, and parents. In our day, this list needs to be expanded. It now includes universities, utility companies, economic structures, multinational corporations, the Internet, the entertainment industry, and news outlets.

It would be almost impossible to cover all the ways that Christians may bear witness to such a wide sampling of powers and principalities. Each one possesses a unique constellation of challenges and opportunities. In this chapter, I focus specifically on state authorities. Though much of what I say about witness to the state applies to other powers, for the sake of space I leave it to readers to make those connections.

At the risk of oversimplifying, I use the term "state" to mean governing authorities and the structures they create to oversee the general affairs of a particular territory or group of people. The state is particularly important to our topic because it is foremost among earthly powers whose divine mandate is to limit disorder and promote the well-being of its citizens. We might go so far as to identify state officials as God's lead agents in making this world a better place.

Church, State, and a Better Place

The state stands in a particular sort of relation to heaven-centered and world-centered approaches to a better place. Since the heaven-centered approach is most concerned with rescuing people from this world and preparing them for the next one, it can be quite indifferent to the state. As far as it is concerned, the state stands at the helm of a sinking ship. It exercises great power in a realm that the heaven-centered view has little stake in preserving. State powers will rise and fall, but only God's eternal kingdom will endure. Because proponents of this view care about people's general well-being and prefer to live in a world at peace, they want the state to be as benevolent and stable as possible. Since they don't trust certain officials to carry out this responsibility, some may even seek governmental power so they can promote laws beneficial to their cause. Still, nothing about this view commits believers to be actively involved with the state.

Because the state possesses more power for social change than any other institution, the world-centered approach cannot be indifferent to it. It is either too valuable an ally or too powerful an opponent to ignore. In many regards, the state and the world-centered church want the same thing. They want to make the world a certain way. They want to shape it according to their vision of what is in everyone's best interests. The world-centered approach thus seeks to cooperate with the state in order to achieve common goals. If poverty is a problem, the church can save a lot of time, money, and energy if it can convince the state to pass legislation that will either solve the problem or provide funding that the church can use to solve it. It makes good sense in terms of stewardship; the church can get more mileage out of its own resources if it can tap into the rich coffers of the state.

The state is important to the world-centered view in another way. What the state leaves undone sets a good deal of the church's agenda. There's no need to duplicate work that the state is already doing quite well. There's no sense meeting needs that someone else is meeting. If the church really wants to improve this world, it should focus its efforts on areas where the state or other public institutions are not adequately helping out.

There are many good reasons for spending time discussing the internal logic of the world-centered and heaven-centered views. I want it to be clear that Christians shouldn't reject these views because they're internally inconsistent. They make perfect sense in light of their own commitments. They may even be sustainable in certain ways. But the ways in which they make sense and the ways in which they are sustainable are not God's way. And that's why we should reject them.

The kingdom-centered view is different. It calls for a unique relationship to the state. Like the heaven-centered view, it recognizes that the state's agenda is not its own. The kingdom-centered church does not work to make this world better; it embraces, displays, and proclaims the better world that God provided precisely to serve as an *alternative* to the fallen order ruled by the state. The difference is not that the state cares about *this* world and the church cares about the *next* one. The difference is that two dominions occupy the same planet in two very different ways. And God's kingdom has already begun to supplant the state's dominion.

The difference between the agenda of the state and that of God's people is most evident when we contrast it with Scripture's teaching about the kingdom.

- God's kingdom takes precedence over all other loyalties; the state asks for allegiance and a willingness to kill and die for it.

- God's kingdom lives by God's wisdom; the state lives by the wisdom of the people and their rulers.

- God's kingdom flees from and repents of immorality; the state tolerates most forms of immorality that don't immediately hurt others.

- God's kingdom shows equality to all people; the state discriminates against citizens of other states, especially those with significantly different political philosophies.

- God's kingdom loves without partiality; the state favors the wealthy and influential.

- God's kingdom unifies through diversity; the state tolerates diversity, but promotes uniformity.

- God's kingdom forgives and reconciles at all levels; the state punishes wrongdoing decisively.

- God's kingdom seeks peace in all circumstances; the state wages war whenever it's politically and economically expedient.

- God's kingdom values childlike humility; the state makes arrogant claims for itself and its agendas.

- God's kingdom exercises leadership through service; the state lords over people.

- God's kingdom esteems small, unimpressive beginnings; the state seeks worldly greatness.

- God's kingdom welcomes the undeserving and unexpected; the state considers them a problem to be dealt with and protected against.

- God's kingdom assimilates the poor more easily than the wealthy; the state esteems the accumulation of wealth and property as one of the highest ideals.

- God's kingdom provides generously for all needs; the state provides selectively according to expediency.

- God's kingdom infiltrates the entire world; the state is concerned primarily with its own territory and invests elsewhere only where positive returns are foreseeable.

- God's kingdom is guided by God's Spirit; the state does not understand God's Spirit and is guided by the power of the air and the spirit of disobedience (Eph 2:2).

- God's kingdom triumphs over persecution, bondage, suffering, and death; the state perpetuates these atrocities when individuals and groups stand in its way.

- God's kingdom raises people to eternal life; the state focuses exclusively on this life.

- God's kingdom acknowledges God's ownership of all life; the state claims sovereignty over human and animal life and takes it when expedient.

- God's kingdom entails a restoration of this earth; the state exploits the earth's resources as much as public opinion will allow.

- God's kingdom judges all powers and personalities counter to God's kingdom; the state is one of these powers and is destined for divine judgment.

In light of these fundamental differences, Christians committed to embracing, displaying, and proclaiming God's kingdom just won't be all that interested in joining the state's efforts to improve this world.

Despite the state's inadequacies, Christians must recognize the important role it plays in God's governance of this world. Though its role is much different from ours, it is nonetheless vital. We therefore appreciate and respect the limited stability and peace that the state is able to achieve. We recognize that the world is a better place because of its work. We pray for the state because we are well aware of its potential to do great good and to inflict great harm. Moreover, the state creates the conditions and context in which we live out our distinct role.

In light of the important service the state renders on God's behalf, the stark differences between God's kingdom and the state lead Christians into a unique stance toward the state. Neither warm embrace, nor hostile resistance will do; instead, our mission requires us to maintain a stance of respectful disentanglement. We gain a helpful perspective on what this might look like by considering how ancient Israel's priests related to the ruling structures of the twelve tribes. This comparison to priests has deep Scriptural roots. It is the first blessing God pronounces over his people in Exodus 19 and it is one of the last labels he applies to them in Revelation 20.[1]

Priestly Irresponsibility

When God brought the Israelites into the land of Canaan, he divided them into twelve territories according to the tribes of Israel. Ten of Jacob's sons inherited one territory each, as did Joseph's two sons. To the twelve tribes with territory, God gave leaders who shared the responsibilities of overseeing property, economics, justice, and other civil affairs (Deut 16–17).

But Levi's descendants—the priests—received no territorial allotment (Num 18:20). They were scattered among Israel's tribes so they might dwell among them in a unique capacity. They focused on studying Torah, administering the sacrificial system, overseeing cities of refuge, signaling when God has declared war against an enemy, leading various festivals, and seeking God's guidance when their host tribe encountered questions to which their leaders could not find clear answers in Torah.[2]

These Levites bore a heavy burden. They had much work to do and they were the only ones who were commissioned to do it. To free them up to focus on their unique responsibilities, God provided others to do the work of everyday governance in their host tribes. The Levites did not

1. Specific references include Exod 19:5–6; 1 Pet 2:4–5; and Rev 1:5–6; 5:10; 20:6.
2. Num 10:8–10; ch. 18; and ch. 35; Deut 31:7–9; 33:8–10.

manage the towns of their host tribes; the elders did that. They did not settle common judicial disputes; the judges did that. They neither went to war when their host tribes were threatened, nor executed capital offenders. There were many aspects of their host tribe's life that they simply did not get involved in. Though their fluency in Torah qualified them more than many tribal leaders, they had to trust that God would meet most of the host tribes' needs without their help.

That trust must have been immensely difficult to cultivate. Though the Levites were relatively disconnected from certain aspects of tribal life, especially its governance, there were significant payoffs for their host tribes. The Levites served an absolutely vital role on their behalf. Since they did not fight Israel's wars, they could impartially discern whether particular wars were divinely sanctioned. Since they did not judge or execute capital criminals, they were able to host killers who sought sanctuary in their cities of refuge until tribal officials could determine innocence or guilt. Because they did not enforce tribal laws and were not closely related to any who may be accused, they were objective enough to take ambiguous cases to God for a definitive ruling. Because they had no official territory of their own, they could help settle boundary disputes. Since the land on which they lived was not truly theirs, they were free to leave it for extended periods in order to serve as needed at the tabernacle. They were able to serve in all of these unique capacities because they were restricted from performing the governing, juridical, and military functions of other Israelites.

Were the Levites being irresponsible in not seeking to involve themselves in the everyday affairs of tribal governance? By no means! On the contrary, they could only be accused of irresponsibility had they abandoned their divinely appointed priestly posts in order to carry out the work of their host tribe's leaders. They could best render the service to which they were called by trusting God to provide others to do all work that lay beyond their purview.[3]

This priestly analogy breaks down at a few important points. Both the Levites and their host tribes were part of the chosen people that God was forming to be a witness to all nations. Both confessed God's rule over every aspect of life. And both were bound to the same Torah.

The church's relation to its host states is quite different. Modern states are not the appointed harbingers of God's new order; they are fallen

---

3. I develop this priestly analogy at greater length in *The Politics of Yahweh*, 191–210.

powers that God uses to uphold the old order. God's chosen people, the church, have been uniquely called to live according to the new order of God's kingdom. Levites could fulfill a chaplain-like function on behalf of other tribes only because they belonged to the same Lord and shared the same values. But that is not how Scripture portrays the church's relationship to the world. God's people are set apart from world powers because they seek a different kingdom, follow a different Lord, and expect a different inheritance when Christ returns.

Despite the differences between their context and ours, there is abundant evidence in Scripture that God's people have a set-apart role analogous to Israel's priests. God has sent us into all nations as aliens and exiles whose citizenship is in heaven. He has done this precisely so we would not attach our identity to our host nations and so we would be properly positioned to serve them in ways that only those who seek first God's kingdom can. Our disentanglement from *running* our host nations frees us up to welcome and assimilate those who are a burden or a threat to our unbelieving neighbors. Such disentanglement also positions us to bear witness to an alternative kingdom that is here in part and will someday come in full. Our priestly "irresponsibility" makes possible our priestly responsibility.

Perhaps this is why God prefaces his covenant-making ceremony with the Israelites after delivering them from Egypt by saying, "Indeed the whole earth is mine, but you shall be for me a priestly kingdom and a holy nation" (Exod 19:5–6). This is why Peter, in the New Testament letter that most accentuates the exilic nature of God's people, echoes Exodus 19 and affirms the priestly status of the church (1 Pet 2:9).

By invoking the example of the Levites, I am not suggesting that the church's only contributions are in the spiritual realm. Consider, for example, how the church's economic practices positively impact wider society. As congregations around the world live out kingdom economics, they will be helping poor people within and around the local church. Keeping fellow believers financially afloat and helping them get on their feet makes them less of a drain on the broader economy. The discipleship that accompanies church support means they will be practicing better stewardship, finding appropriate work, beginning to help others, and learning not to cheat on their taxes. All of this benefits society at large. As believers take the godly economic practices they have learned from Scripture and apply them in the workforce, that will also have positive economic ramifications. It is not a top-down influence on the wider economy, but it is a substantial influence that makes a positive contribution to the common good.

Similar things can be said about other aspects of public life. The church didn't wait for the state to act before starting up the first hospitals and Sunday schools. They observed that only the well-to-do had access to quality healthcare and education, and they began serving their immediate communities by doing what they could *as the church* and with the resources of the Christian community.

This witness had a positive impact on wider society. It raised awareness of specific needs and eventually prompted unbelievers to consider how they, too, might contribute to the health and education of all people. This is part of what it means for the church to be salt, light, and leaven. We do what we do because God has called us to do it. We serve with the bottom-up power that Christ infused in us, and we trust God to grow the seeds that we plant.

This priestly analogy demonstrates that Christians who choose not to get deeply entangled in the political affairs of their host nations are not simply lazy, unloving, or irresponsible. Nor are they attempting to dishonor the blood that was shed by those who fought to establish the various nations we live in today. They are honoring the blood that Christ shed, as well as those Christian martyrs who followed in his steps. These martyrs traded worldly domination for the reign of God and, by refusing to worship the rulers of the nations, bore witness to the transterritorial eternal kingdom of which we are now a part.

Since the mission of God's people entails forming communities that embody Jesus' alternative all-encompassing politics precisely *for the world's sake*, then focusing on our mission is not lazy, unloving, irresponsible, or ungrateful. It is rightly ordered action, love, responsibility, and gratitude. Since it is God's strategy for blessing all nations, it is the best way to preserve whatever is good and worth dying for in this world. Those who reject God's strategy or merge it with the world's strategies by making yet another pointless run at ruling like the nations are the ones who are acting irresponsibly.

Principles for Witnessing to the State

There are multiple ways the church may witness to the state while focusing on being the better place that God has created in this world through Jesus.

By being a better place, the church is a visible sign of God's control of world history through Christ. Though the state often appears to control world history, it does not. God has exalted Jesus to his right hand and all powers are being placed under his feet. Their rule is not a complete sham, but they control a diminishing realm with little future. So we don't need to fret over cyclical elections that promise a future they cannot deliver or pose a threat that is not ultimate. We see through all rhetoric which claims that voting a particular person, platform, or party into office will somehow change everything and set this world straight. We don't panic over territorial skirmishes that promise to end conflict, but usually only escalate it. This world's structures are useful to God and accomplish his limited purposes for them, but they are not all that they appear to be.

By being a better place, the church reminds the state that it is not the only institution that commands loyalty. The same God that gives the state its mandate has authorized the church to play an important role, indeed the most important role in world history. Insofar as it follows the Lord of history and serves as the firstfruits of the world to come, the church bears the meaning and direction of world history. By being fiercely loyal to our church family, Christians help the state keep its limited power in proper perspective. Its power is on loan from God, as is its limited authority over the lives of its citizens. We neither envy its power nor covet its influence because our role is clear—and it differs from that of the state.

By being a better place, the church reminds the state that it is not God's agent for saving this world, but for maintaining a basic level of order and seeking the good of its citizens. Just as it is tempting for the church to mistake its important role in God's plan for license to rule the world, it is tempting for the state to mistake its important role in maintaining order for license to try to save the world by ushering in a new utopian world order. The church's witness to God's kingdom thus helps keep in check any state that naïvely and foolishly covets absolute sway over all creation. The cosmos already has a Lord; his name is Jesus.

By being a better place, the church reminds the state that God cares about all people and not just those who live in their particular territory. Since the church represents God's new humanity—which is comprised of people from all ethnicities, countries, and continents—it reminds the state that people created in God's image are scattered all throughout the world and are not limited to the confines of its jurisdiction. So God is not necessarily on any state's side, though we might say that states that serve the best interests of all creat ion, all humans, and all nonhuman creatures are closer to being on God's side.

By being a better place, the church reminds the state that God's kingdom is the standard for all things, and that the way of Jesus is possible in world history. The ability to establish laws that all citizens must obey often leads governing authorities to think they know what is in everyone's best interests. This, they believe, entitles them to lord it over their subjects. Yet Jesus came serving and not lording over his people. As the co-creator and Lord of *all* creation, he alone knows what is best. His people keep alive his vision for human thriving whether the state adheres to it or not.

By being a better place, the church equips its members to live out the way of Christ in every aspect of their lives, whether at work, church, school, home, or in the marketplace. Since many believers serve within state agencies, they bring the wisdom of God's kingdom to bear on state affairs. Some state officials will notice this wisdom and embrace it as well. To the extent that they do, the church helps make the state a better state.

By being a better place, the church equips its members to honor state officials by praying for them and for all who are impacted by their policies. We will pray for them whether they are humble or vain, effective or defective, righteous or wicked, deserving or unworthy. Our *respectful* disentanglement positions us to see them for what they truly are. At their best they are well-intentioned people who want to make the world a better place. Still, they must contend with human hearts that, since the time of Noah's flood, remain always evil all the time (Gen 6:5). They cannot succeed in ushering in an ultimate order of peace, for God has already ushered in his peaceful kingdom, and they didn't have eyes to see it or ears to hear it. We should pray for them. Their social engineering dreams are doomed to dissolve, but their work nonetheless has strong short-term influence on the lives of all people and the conditions in which all churches carry out their mission.

23

Conclusion

THE CHURCH NEEDS A more biblical vision of a better place than the
various versions espoused today. God has not called the church to prepare people for a better place somewhere else (heaven-centered view).
He never authorized us to make this world better through human effort
(human-centered view). Nor did God begin refashioning this world into
a better place and then call the church to continue to improve it in anticipation of the whole world's redemption when Christ returns (world-
centered view).

· None of these approaches are fully Christian because none of them
fits the role God has assigned his people in Scripture. In order to gain a
better sense of that role, we rehearsed the Bible's story of a better place
from beginning to end. In doing so, we saw that God created this world to
be a very good place for all his creatures. We saw that humans corrupted
God's very good place with sin and unbridled violence. Sensing that creation was on the brink of self-destruction, God intervened decisively. He
minimized the impact of violence by purging the earth of nearly all living
creatures, shortening human life-spans, safeguarding all lifeblood, and
placing limits on vengeance. God then kick-started the diversification of
human cultures so that no single culture, however powerful, could force
its way of life on all people. This was the beginning of God's use of the
powers and principalities to make this world a significantly better place.

As crucial as all these measures were, they could not generate a
culture of flourishing and peace between God, humans, and nonhuman
creation. Under the powers' administration, life on earth was far more
tolerable, but not nearly the very good place God created it to be. So

God devised a strategy to offer abundant life to all humans without over-riding the option he gave them to live as they see fit. Beginning with Abraham, he formed a set-apart people to prepare this world for a better place. God sought to order the life of Abraham's descendants according to the better way set forth in Torah. God intended to use this better way to bless all nations. Yet God's people were not patient with this strategy. They devised other plans. They wanted to be impressive and powerful like other nations, so they merged God's ways with theirs. This was not going to accomplish God's purpose for his people, so he humbled them, stripped them of their vain achievements, and left them with no hope except for him.

God promised his people through the prophets that he was far from finished with his broken world. He planned to return to them in Spirit and in power. He would gather his wayward people, heal his sick cre-ation, and usher in an era of prosperity that would attract and eventually assimilate all nations into his global reign of justice. This earth would become the better place for which God's people had been waiting. When the fullness of time had come, God sent Jesus to inaugurate this better place. Jesus spoke of it mostly in terms of God's kingdom. It was the cen-ter of his gospel message.

Jesus implemented God's kingdom in a way that no one expected. Rather than *replace* the corrupt structures of the fallen world order, Jesus began his new order right in the midst of the old one. He gathered his people, awakened them to newness of life, infused them with his Spirit, and sent them on a mission. This newness of life was not a minor tweak to life as usual. It signaled a new era in world history, a new world reality, a new way of living, a new way of relating to people, a new people to relate to, a new status before God and all creation, and a life of abundant blessings.

The kingdom is an indescribable gift that seems too good to believe. Perhaps more difficult to believe is that God has entrusted this gift to his fragile people. He called an undeserving community with a poor track record to bear the meaning and direction of world history. By faith we must embrace this gift, display it in our life together, and proclaim it to the whole world. In Christ, God has accomplished this, but he has chosen to make his appeal through us. We are the only ambassadors God has appointed to represent his eternal kingdom. We carry in our life together the fullness of life that prophets have envisioned, kings have striven to achieve, angels having been longing to observe, and creation groans to experience.

This story, of course, is not complete. Though God's kingdom operates powerfully among God's people, God has been patient with those who deny its coming. Wanting all to embrace his reign, he has allowed rebellious powers to continue their rule for a time. Yet God will not tarry forever. He will return, eliminate all powers that oppose him, restore all creation, fulfill what remains of Israel's hopes, and raise to eternal life on a renewed earth all who died seeking first his kingdom. God will make this world the very best place he always intended it to be.

Having walked through this story, we were then prepared to articulate the specific relationship between the church and God's better place: the church's role is to *be the better place* that God has already made in this world. I call this a "kingdom-centered" approach because our role centers on embracing, displaying, and proclaiming God's kingdom. This approach does not want something different from most other Christian views. It, too, wants this world to be the best possible place. It cares deeply about the deterioration of creation and the suffering of countless people. It remains "kingdom" centered because it believes that God's people have been re-created as the firstfruits of the best possible place, which is God's kingdom. God has appointed us—and no one else—to serve this kingdom. We are the frontrunners of world history. Why would we be distracted by even the most noble alternative vision? Why shift our focus to making a fading world order as good as it can be before it eventually bottoms out?

The kingdom-centered approach not only flows from the overall direction of the Bible story, but it also makes better sense of core Christian practices than the other approaches we've considered. It resonates deeply with Scripture's teaching on communal practices like discipleship, leadership, fellowship, kinship, and friendship. Though these practices emphasize that believers must prioritize the kingdom community, this does not mean we should withdraw from all unbelievers and may take no part in activities that make this fallen world better. Our discussion of vocation, missions, and witness to the powers makes clear that being God's better place must not lead to social isolation. God has made his people a better place precisely so we may extend that offer to others. Intentional, meaningful contact with unbelievers is therefore essential.

Pitfalls to Avoid

Churches committed to being God's better place must be careful to avoid two pitfalls. The first is *isolationism*. Isolationism occurs when the church completely withdraws from the world, regardless of its reasons for doing so. Such insularity is wrong-minded because Christian witness and mission demand serious engagement with the wider world. Churches that cease to exist for the world cease to exist as an integral part of God's plan.

We should not, however, mistake prioritization for isolationism. God's mission requires us to love one another fervently, and that should be obvious in how we spend our time, energy, and resources. If we have read the Bible story correctly, then it is not insular to prioritize the family of God *or* to claim that we are the new humanity *or* to downplay the notion that we must make this world better. It's just biblical.

To prioritize one another in this way is not insular if a new world order has truly begun in Jesus and God has called us to boldly represent it. God cares for this world far more than any human ever has, and God has seen from his infinitely superior vantage point that our love for one another is the best possible approach for drawing all people to himself. Our response is obedience. Committing ourselves to learning how to love one another is our faithful and effective witness.

Jesus' mustard seed analogy helps us understand the logic behind God's plan: "With what can we compare the kingdom of God, or what parable will we use for it? It is like a mustard seed, which, when sown upon the ground, is the smallest of all the seeds on earth; yet when it is sown it grows up and becomes the greatest of all shrubs, and puts forth large branches, so that the birds of the air can make nests in its shade" (Mark 4:30–32).

The kingdom is God's plant. It's a seedling, and it starts small. It grows inconspicuously in the orchard of the world. But it is growing. And it will become so prominent that all creatures will find refuge in its shade.

When the plant is still small and weak, it looks like a weed. It's easy to dismiss. It might even seem petty to focus on nourishing it. After all, there are larger plants in the orchard that already provide some shade. Plus, we only have so much water, fertilizer, and energy to spare.

But we know better. God has put us "in the know" and called us his friends. We know that the larger plants are destined to wither and that this small shoot will grow up. We know that this little plant is the only one that will sustain all creatures indefinitely. So we know that it's not petty or insular to prioritize it, but the opposite. God is making it grow, and God has asked us to water it. To fulfill this request, even at the expense of other plants, is the only faithful response.

Utopianism is another pitfall. Utopian communities naively or impractically attempt to create an ideal society. They believe they have identified the perfect social formula and that implementing it will generate a community of prosperity and tranquility—the likes of which this world has never seen.

Christian communities can get caught up in utopianism in various ways. This happens when church members live as if the fall's negative effects no longer impact their lives. Communities that don't strive to maintain healthy boundaries to guard against sin are utopian insofar as they act as if believers were sinless and beyond temptation. The same can be said of communities that affirm that all of God's promises for this world have already been fulfilled or that humans can actually bring heaven to earth instead of receiving the kingdom as solely God's accomplishment. These sorts of utopian visions need to be avoided. The kingdom-centered view needs to avoid them just as much as the human- and world-centered views.

It is not utopian, however, for Christian communities to cast a vision of a better future. Israel's prophets did that (Isa 65:17–25). It's not utopian to live now in light of one's hope for a better future. The New Testament extols Israel's heroes for doing that (Heb 11). It's not naïve or utopian to presume that we are already firsthand participants in God's better place. That is a matter of faith that we share with Jesus (Luke 4:18–21), the early church (Jas 1:18; 1 John 2:8), and God's good creation (Rom 8:19).

A New View of Reality

Even after acknowledging certain pitfalls to avoid, the kingdom-centered approach set forth in this book will be hard for some to accept. We've had over a millennium of cordial partnerships with the prevailing world powers. This experience has either crushed all our hopes for this world *or* conditioned us to think that our most noble contribution to world history is to make life as pleasant as it can be for as many people as possible by striving to make this world a better place. You may recall that these two options overlap considerably with the four Jewish options Jesus encountered and rejected, those of the Zealots, Essenes, Pharisees, and Sadducees.

Christ rejected their ways because they weren't God's way for his people. He called them to repent, die to their old selves, and be reborn. The Apostle Paul said it best: "If anyone is in Christ, there is a new creation" (2 Cor 5:17). Believers of all stripes recognize their newness in Christ. We sing songs about being born again and leaving our old lives behind. By this we usually mean forgiveness of sins, a fresh start, a better life rhythm, a sense of purpose, and hope for resurrection.

The Apostle Paul goes further. Conversion impacts not only God's view of us and our view of ourselves, but also our view of the cosmos and our understanding of the meaning and direction of world history. We enter into a new awareness and a new way of interacting with everyone and everything around us.

The newness Paul envisions is similar to what we encounter in the 1999 blockbuster film, *The Matrix*. In this sci-fi thriller, the world is not what it appears to be, though most humans think they are living normal lives. They think they are eating and drinking, playing and working under the blue sky and bright sun with family, friends, and co-workers. But Neo, the lead character, must learn that this perception of reality is an illusion. It is a false world being pulled over his eyes.

In reality, machines had taken over the world. For the sake of energy, they harvest humans in vast fields of hibernation pods that supply them with power. To channel and subdue humanity's thirst for genuine life, they create a computer-simulated world that closely resembles life as humans once knew it. They then plug human brains into this world, known as the Matrix, and people dream their way through life in the artificial reality created by the machines.

In this dystopian reality, conversion to new life means waking up from the machine-induced slumber. It means confessing that the Matrix is not reality. The real world is run by machines, and humans merely serve as highly evolved energy sources. In this story world, conversion means more than a change in self-perception. It means waking up to an entirely different vision of reality. It means unplugging from the Matrix and seeing all things for what they truly are.

Scripture speaks of conversion in similar terms. It means new birth to a new world reality. We no longer view anything or anyone from a human point of view. We view everything in light of God's kingdom as revealed in Jesus.

The Gospel

At its core, this new world reality is gospel: it's good news of God's gift. Humans did nothing to bring God's kingdom and can do nothing to stop it. God's gift is not otherworldly, but very much this-worldly. It is neither entirely future nor fully realized in the present. It began with the first coming of Christ and will be completed when he returns. It is not work that we must accomplish, but the result of work that God has already accomplished for us. What remains for us to do is to embrace, display, and proclaim God's gracious gift. This is, indeed, good news, and it's what a broken world desperately needs to hear.

It is good news for those who are striving to save themselves and atone for past failings through moral purity, spiritual discipline, or fervent philanthropy. We need not atone for sin or save ourselves because God has already done so through Christ.

It is good news for those who are striving to fix their nations through tactical alliances with the powers and principalities. We need not fix our nations because Jesus is their Lord and not us, and he is able to use them for his purposes without our help and in spite of their inadequacies.

It is good news for those who are striving to grow their churches to respectable sizes through sleek marketing and cutting-edge programming. We need not grow our churches at all because God's role for us does not require a particular size and Scripture clearly teaches that God is responsible for church growth and not us (1 Cor 3:6–7; Col 2:19).

It is good news for those who are striving to raise perfect families by maintaining rigorous boundaries and enforcing strict regimens. We need not raise perfect families because God doesn't need our perfect families and because he has already adopted us into his wider family of believers.

It was tempting for me to say that we "need not *and cannot*" save ourselves, that we "need not *and cannot*" fix our nations, that we "need not *and cannot*" grow our churches, that we "need not *and cannot*" raise perfect families. But that is not entirely true.

When primeval civilization sought to accomplish an amazing feat by building a mighty city reaching into the heavens, God did not say, "they cannot do it." Instead he confessed, "Look, they are one people, and they all have one language; and this is only the beginning of what they will do; nothing that they propose to do will now be impossible for them" (Gen 11:6).

And so it is with us. If enough of God's people truly believe in a good cause and are truly united in championing it together, there is nothing we cannot do. So the problem with striving to save ourselves, trying to fix our nations, trying to grow our churches, and trying to raise perfect families is not that we *cannot* do it. The problem is that we *could*. The salvation we achieve, the nations we fix, the churches we grow, and the families we raise would be truly impressive. They would represent the best that hardworking humans can do when they put their minds to something. They may even feel like new creation, newness of life, and new humanity. They may indeed make this world a better place, and no one would be able to deny it.

But it wouldn't be the gospel of Jesus Christ. It wouldn't be *God's* kingdom. It wouldn't be the best possible place that God has for us. Jesus would not have had to give his life on our behalf. God would not have had to send his Spirit to empower us. The apostles would have spent their lives in vain. God would have dramatically intervened in world history only to ask his people to do what human potential with the proper motivation was already able to do.

If we wish to participate in the very best place that God has in store for creation, then let us *become*, as a people, the better place that Christ has created us to be. Let us receive the gift of God's reign. It's here. It's growing. It's how God is saving the world.

Bibliography

Blackburn, Bradley. "The Giving Pledge: Billionaires Promise to Donate at Least Half Their Fortunes to Charity." ABC News (August 4, 2010). http://abcnews.go.com/WN/bill-gates-warren-buffett-organize-billionaire-giving-pledge/story?id=11325984.

Dutton, Marsha L., ed. *Aelred of Rievaulx: Spiritual Friendship*. Cistercian Studies Series. Trappist, KY: Cistercian, 2010.

Edmonds, Molly. "What is Friendship?" http://people.howstuffworks.com/what-is-friendship.htm (accessed May 29, 2015).

Grinberg, Emanuella, and John Couwels. "Manatees Set for Removal from U.S. Endangered Species List." http://www.cnn.com/2016/01/08/living/manatee-endangered-species-feat.

Hill, Wesley. *Spiritual Friendship: Finding Love in the Church as a Celibate Gay Christian*. Grand Rapids: Zondervan, 2015.

Hunter, James Davison. *To Change the World: The Irony, Tragedy, & Possibility of Christianity in the Late Modern World*. New York: Oxford University Press, 2010.

Keller, Tim. "Leadership and Church Size Dynamics: How Strategy Changes with Growth." In *The Movement Newsletter* (2006). http://www.livingwatercc.org/images/VarArticles/ChurchSize2.pdf.

Lohfink, Gerhard. *Jesus and Community: The Social Dimension of Christian Faith*. Philadelphia: Fortress, 1984.

McKnight, Scot. *Kingdom Conspiracy: Returning to the Radical Mission of the Local Church*. Grand Rapids: Brazos, 2014.

McNeal, Reggie. *Kingdom Come: Why We Must Give Up Our Obsession with Fixing the Church and What We Should Do Instead*. Carol Stream, IL: Tyndale Momentum, 2015.

Middleton, J. Richard. *A New Heaven and a New Earth: Reclaiming Biblical Eschatology*. Grand Rapids: Baker Academic, 2014.

Nugent, John C. "Kingdom Work: John Howard Yoder's Free Church Contributions to an Ecumenical Theology of Vocation." In *Radical Ecumenicity: Pursuing Unity and Continuity after John Howard Yoder*, edited by John C. Nugent, 149–172. Abilene, TX: Abilene Christian University Press, 2010.

———. *The Politics of Yahweh: John Howard Yoder, the Old Testament, and the People of God*. Eugene, OR: Cascade, 2011.

Pennington, Jonathan T. *Heaven and Earth in the Gospel of Matthew*. Grand Rapids: Baker Academic, 2007.

Rauschenbusch, Walter. *A Theology for the Social Gospel*. Louisville: Westminster John Knox, 1997.

Snyder, Howard A. *Salvation Means Creation Healed: The Ecology of Sin and Grace: Overcoming the Divorce Between Heaven and Earth*. Eugene, OR: Cascade, 2011.

Wright, N. T. *Surprised by Hope: Rethinking Heaven, the Resurrection, and the Mission of the Church*. New York: HarperOne, 2008.

APPENDIX

Answers to Practical Questions

Struggling with Your Church

1. I am part of a progressive church that wants to save this world. How is a kingdom-centered approach good news for my church?

Any church that is trying to save the world doesn't fully grasp the good news of Jesus. The gospel that Christians have been commissioned to embrace, display, and proclaim is that in Christ God has already begun to save the world. He has done so by building a new world in the midst of the old one. God has already reconciled all things to himself through Christ, and our role is to serve as ambassadors of that new world. For those who are in Christ, all things are already new. We no longer view anyone from a human point of view. All things are already ours in Christ (1 Cor 3:21-23).

The good news is that the world doesn't need us to save it. This is actually great news because we are lousy world savers. In fits and spurts we can do some good. But all human efforts to save the world are doomed to fail. Daniel 2 gives us a wonderful illustration of why. It depicts a statue made of layers of different metals, each of which represents a worldly kingdom that rises to power for a limited time. Yet all of them are replaced by a rock that is carved out "not by human hands" (v. 34). This is the kingdom that Christ brought. Any kingdom built by human hands cannot be the kingdom of Christ. Like the foolish man who built his house upon the sand, it may seem impressive for a time but it will come tumbling down when the cultural political climate changes (Matt 7:24-27). Ultimately, it will be supplanted when Christ returns to finalize his kingdom and destroy all human kingdoms—even those that humans build in his name (1 Cor 15:24).

It is also good news for progressive Christians who have been trying to save the world and are learning that they can't. They are tired of failing and frustrated with other believers who won't join them. Some are on the brink of forsaking the faith altogether because there is no success in sight. It is good news that they are only failing at something that they were never called to do. Yet there is a commission in which they can succeed! They can embrace, display, and proclaim God's kingdom. They need not even do so perfectly for God's plan to succeed.

2. I am a part of an inwardly focused church that mostly ignores the outer world. How is a kingdom-centered approach good news for my church?

A church that does not exist for the world does not exist as the church. Our mission to the world is our lifeblood. It's why we exist. So the good news for an inwardly focused church is that it may still become the bride of Christ. Churches become self-absorbed for various reasons. Sometimes they turn inward because all of their prior outward efforts have revolved around trying to fix the world. Having failed at this task, they then retreat. The good news is that their failure at this does not condemn them. There was no way they could succeed. It wasn't their job, and God didn't empower them to do it. The good news is that they can rethink their approach to the world. They can center it on God's mission and they can succeed at embracing, displaying, and proclaiming his kingdom. They may find it extremely refreshing to approach the world as gift-givers and gospel proclaimers. They may draw energy from asking new questions like, "How can we as a church body creatively show our community what God's kingdom is like?"

3. I am not the pastor of a church. How do I get my church to see its central importance in God's mission? How do I get my church on the "abundant life together" track?

To begin with, we may relieve ourselves of the burden of fixing our church. It's not our church; it's God's church. What we have to offer the world is a gift, and what we have to extend to one another is a gift—the same gift. For many of us who have spent too much time trying to engineer a better world, it is tempting to take the same mind-set into the church: how can we engineer a better church? But that is God's role, not ours. We are fellow beggars who have bread to share. So we can start by sharing our bread, loving one another, opening our homes to lonely members, opening our purses to needy church members, involving others in our family celebrations, confessing our sins, and reconciling with estranged brothers and sisters in Christ. We can start by being an example and living the life to which all members are called.

The gospel is contagious. So we should befriend fellow members who haven't quite embraced God's kingdom and begin mentoring them in the faith. We should pray fervently for fellow believers and even leaders who don't quite get it. But like Jesus taught, we must not elevate ourselves (Luke 14:7–11). We shouldn't imagine that change happens in the church like it does in the world. We shouldn't assume that we have to become powerful leaders who can enforce God's kingdom from the top. Instead, we must sit at the foot of the table and serve. If God wants to give us more influence, he will. We won't have to engineer it. We must serve faithfully where we are. We can impact those who already respect us without coveting the influence that others may have. We can trust God's Spirit to guide our next step. We must not get puffed up, but serve humbly. When given the opportunity, we can share the reasons for our actions. We can proclaim the kingdom in words and extend the kingdom invitation to others.

4. The kingdom-centered approach you recommend doesn't match my church or any of the churches near me. How do I find one?

We need not wait for the perfect church to come along. We can often start right where we are. We can start being a member who treats church family like real family. We can start turning "church friends" into real friends. Many churches encourage members to be a part of small groups where life is shared more intimately. We should join such groups and begin building relationships that display God's kingdom. I have yet to encounter a church leader who would discourage people from truly loving fellow members and prioritizing God's kingdom.

Those who are not already part of a church family should begin their inquiry with the same mind-set. The perfect church doesn't exist, so there is little use in waiting for one. God's treasure was meant to be carried in clay jars (2 Cor 4:7). The weakness of the messenger does not negate the strength of the message. The reality is, there can be no such thing as a perfect church. A church that fulfills its responsibility attracts new people. When new people come, they bring all of their imperfections with them. So the church is constantly in the process of helping imperfect people who do not yet seek first God's kingdom to begin seeking it first.

5. *Church just isn't for me. I've been burned before and I'm really more of an introvert anyway. Are you saying there is no place in God's kingdom for me?*

I deeply sympathize with those who have been hurt by other Christians. It is extremely difficult to trust people who have wounded us. Still, God's mission requires it. The kingdom calling is a calling to reconciliation. It is the ministry of bringing together people whose lives have been torn apart by sin. It is the formation of teams of people whose life together displays the kingdom. A person cannot do that alone. In the kingdom there is no "team of one," regardless of how pure and noble that one may be.

In chapter 15, I used the metaphor of an athletic team. One cannot play in Major League Baseball without being on a team, showing up for practice, following the instruction of coaches, and fielding a position that relates to other players in specific ways. Likewise, a rose cannot be a bouquet of flowers all by itself. A kernel cannot be a cornucopia. A shard of clay is not a mosaic. And so an individual cannot, apart from the wider family of God, display God's kingdom.

This is not to say that all believers must be extroverts. A key attribute of the kingdom is that it is made up of all sorts of people. It requires a variety of gifts and personalities. Not all people are alike, and not all will play the same role. If a congregation has no place for introverts, it needs to rethink the nature of God's kingdom. God's kingdom does not press everyone into a common mold; it binds different people together in a common family.

Sometimes a church doesn't seem like it's for us because of unfaithfulness in that church. In such cases, reconciliation is the goal. God needs good people to stick around long enough to foster repentance and generate positive change. Other times a church doesn't seem like it's for us because we aren't for the church. We expect the church to cater to our expectations even when those expectations don't align with God's kingdom. In such cases, it is we who must change and then give the church another chance. As stated above, there is no perfect church—only imperfect people aspiring to a kingdom that is beyond our ability and maturity. So we must start small and go slow. God is faithful. He gives good gifts to his children. He doesn't want to leave anyone out. If we earnestly desire to join his family, he will work harder than anyone to make a way.

Helping Those Outside the Church

6. Should Christians help those in need who are outside of the church? If so, how?

Though it is not the church's job to fix all social ills, our faithful presence in this world should help unbelievers in a variety of ways. The first way that we help them is by helping one another. Our love for one another shows the world that there are, indeed, people who help one another out. We don't help one another in the paternalistic ways that some philanthropic organizations do. We don't help one another as projects or clients. Nor do we help one another for pay, to feel good about ourselves, or to find meaning in life. We help one another out as equal sharers in God's abundance. If people outside the church don't encounter us as a kingdom people whom they, too, may join—then we haven't helped them out in the most fundamental way that God has called us to help them.

Beyond that, we will also help unbelievers as we go about life in this world. Like the Good Samaritan, we will see people in need, we will have the means to help them, and we will lend a helping hand. We will do good to all people, but especially the family of believers (Gal 6:10). We will do good to all people because the kingdom is like that. In serving one another, we will acquire the ability to serve with excellence and we will take that skill set wherever we go. We will serve with excellence at all times. We will help people in our jobs, in our neighborhoods, within our families, and along our path while we are out and about.

But we will not make helping them the center of our lives. The kingdom is our center. Ideally, we want them to see the help we render to them as the overflow of the help we have received in Christ. Because we are committed first to the family of believers, we will pour constantly into one another's lives. When all members do this, our cup overflows. As our cup overflows, there will be plenty to share with others. We want our help to overflow into the lives of unbelievers so they, too, can taste and see the Lord's goodness. Helping unbelievers is not the problem, helping people in ways that are disconnected from God's strategy for drawing all people to himself is the problem.

7. How should I be compassionate to my needy neighbors outside the church? Should there be limits to my compassion?

Scripture tells us to do good to and honor *all people* (Gal 6:10; 1 Pet 2:17). So we should be good neighbors. We should lend a helping hand and invite people over for supper. We shouldn't do this in order to fix them or the world. They must not become our project. Rather our goodness to them should overflow from the love we show to one another and point back to that love. It *must* point to that love because they will know we are Christian by our love for one another (John 13:35). I am not suggesting that anyone stop being neighborly to unbelievers; I am suggesting that we anchor our neighborliness more firmly in the particular mission God has given us.

Because God's kingdom teaches us that it is better to give than to receive, we would rather serve our needy neighbor than sit at home and stare at our big screens and miniature handheld devices. Because we exist to embrace, display, and proclaim God's kingdom before the watching world, we must take every opportunity to do so. When our neighbors invite us into their lives, we will be humbled by the opportunity and make the most of it (Eph 5:15–16). When we have the opportunity to invite them into our homes, we should do the same. People come to know God's kingdom by seeing it in and among us. We should do whatever we can to increase the visible surface area *of God's kingdom*.

This does not mean that we serve people only to win them over. Like Jesus, we should have compassion on others because they are worthy of our compassion. We should honor them because they, too, are made in God's image and are worthy of honor. We should serve them because that is the natural reflex of kingdom people. It is our habit to drop what we are doing and serve a fellow believer in need, and we want to do the same for neighbors in need. We won't all of a sudden turn on the "witness to the kingdom" switch when a neighbor calls. Our life is a perpetual witness to the kingdom, so we should answer the call and just be ourselves.

Being ourselves also means not being alone. It is often the case that we would be able to better help our neighbor if we were to bring along others in the body who may also be able to help. We can serve our neighbors together when such opportunities present themselves and that would increase the visibility of our love for one another. Of course, there will be times when our neighbor won't want the help of a stranger, so our church friends may not be welcome. We should be sensitive to this and careful not to present our help in a way that would not be received as a gift.

8. Is God at work in nonbelievers who make this world a better place by feeding the hungry, healing the sick, and welcoming strangers?

God is at work all throughout the world. All creation belongs to him. All powers remain under his jurisdiction. Scripture frequently testifies to God's work outside the body of Christ. God uses Egypt to provide for the wider region during a time of great famine. He uses Babylon to punish Assyria. He uses Persian kings to finance Israel's return from exile. He uses parents of believers *and* unbelievers to provide for young children. God may even empower unbelievers by his Spirit to accomplish amazing things that they could not do on their own. We do not know the full extent of God's work in this world, but we trust that he cares more about the needy than any well-intentioned Christian and that he uses a wide array of resources to provide for them.

We must not assume, however, that just because God is doing something we should get in on the action. God has not made the church stewards of all creation. We are stewards of the gospel. Whether we like it or not, worldly powers rule the nations, not us. As Romans 13 makes clear, their work is God's work, too. We rejoice in the good work that public officials and private humanitarians do. Their good deeds stand as a humbling reminder that we are not God's only servants. So, yes, God works through unbelievers, and they accomplish important things. We should value and appreciate that work, but not covet work that has not been given to us.

9. I work in a nonprofit or government organization unaffiliated with the church. How should I understand my work and passion to help non-Christians in need?

As discussed in chapter 20, our particular employment can be of great service to wider society. Yet regardless of our occupation, we are called to seek first God's kingdom. Any good work we do at the office or anywhere else does not save us or anyone else. Only God saves people, and he saves us into his kingdom. He welcomes us into his kingdom work. When we work for the kingdom, we serve ultimate ends; when we work for the powers, we serve penultimate or secondary ends. That said, even work among the powers may point to the kingdom. It does so to the extent that fellow workers see and experience us embracing, displaying, and proclaiming God's reign.

But if it is God's kingdom that they are experiencing, they must see it as different from the kingdom they serve at work. They must see it as a pearl and a treasure that they may embrace only after leaving their old life behind (Matt 13:44-46). For the people we encounter at work to see God's kingdom in us, they will have to see that our work among the powers does not come first in our lives. Our commitment to the kingdom must not be fueled by energy and passion that is left over from our jobs. Our service at work should be fueled by the excess of energy and passion that overflows from our witness to God's kingdom as a part of God's people. Our primary calling is to God's kingdom. Everything else finds its position in relation to it. Any occupation that will not allow us to position it beneath our commitment to God's kingdom cannot be an occupation to which God has called us. Otherwise, we are not seeking God's kingdom first (Matt 6:33). And a house that is divided against itself cannot stand (Mark 3:25).

10. How might a kingdom-centered approach impact the way churches support specific missions, missionaries, and parachurch organizations?

God equips every congregation for the specific work to which he calls it. Though all are called to embrace, display, and proclaim his kingdom, each one does so in ways that are specific to its time and place. So matters of budget and stewardship must be decided on the local church level, in the context of any wider denominational affiliations. Nonetheless, kingdom-centered churches should operate with priorities that are rooted in their understanding of God's mission.

First and foremost, we must make sure that all needs within our local body are met. We are not truly loving one another if this is not the case. Likewise, we should eagerly support whatever persons or organizations supply our church with valuable resources and leaders that empower our mission. To neglect them is akin to dishonoring our parents. Like the Apostle Paul, we should also be mindful of churches that we are affiliated with that are struggling to get by—whether nearby or far away. If God has supplied all of our needs, we should certainly bless them with our excess.

Beyond these immediate connections, the global church and worldwide philanthropic community presents us with endless opportunities to support their work. How might we prioritize among them? Since unbelieving institutions enjoy widespread support from the unbelieving community, it seems appropriate for believers to prioritize organizations that are dedicated to accomplishing God's mission for God's people in God's way. God's way centers on filling every community of this world with churches that embrace, display, and proclaim his kingdom. Organizations that empower and fulfill that work should be our focus. Such organizations are far less likely to enjoy the support of wealthy philanthropists beyond the church.

Jesus instructs us that where our treasure is, our heart will be as well (Matt 6:21). The church budget should thus be a natural extension of our central passion. Since we don't exist to fix this world, neither does our budget. This doesn't mean that we will never give to causes outside of direct kingdom witness. After all, we sometimes serve in causes outside of direct kingdom witness. Since such causes are a secondary part of our life together, they may also occupy a secondary place in our budget.

Taking Social Justice Seriously

11. In an era of globalism, where more needs are known and God's people are able to do more, how should we help those in serious need—like countries experiencing grave injustices?

Though we may only recently be aware of the vastness of human need in this world, God has always known. And, still, his strategy was to fill the earth with communities that embrace, display, and proclaim his kingdom. For the unbelieving powers, this influx of information may lead to a more strategic global approach to philanthropy. God has used and will continue to use such opportunities and resources for good. He will continue to use the powers to make this world a better place by promoting the good and keeping evil in check.

Kingdom-minded people will use this knowledge differently because we have a different commission with different priorities. Global awareness enables us to identify areas in need so we may plant churches there and demonstrate the gospel to them. It also allows us to communicate more easily with churches in need and consider how those with plenty may come alongside and support them. Increased information about this world does not warrant a change in gospel or mission. New knowledge means new resources to convey the gospel and carry out our mission, not a new calling to a rival vision of world betterment.

12. Isn't it irresponsible to say we don't have to work for justice outside the church since we benefit from injustice by living in a privileged time, country, and social position?

Responsibility is a tricky thing. Humans are good at assuming responsibility that has not been given to us and coveting what is not ours. In the world of comic books and empire-building, greater power means greater responsibility. In the world of Scripture, greater status means greater temptation to assume responsibility for making the world a better place. Yet responsibility can only be entrusted to us from someone to whom it already belongs. It must be delegated by someone above us who is ultimately responsibly.

The powerful of this world assume that they are God's gift to the world. They think that their wealth and resources make them responsible for those who have less. But that is not how the Bible talks about responsibility. The Bible states that God presides over all creation. He alone is ultimately responsible. It then states that God allots responsibility as he sees fit. God has indeed placed a good deal of responsibility upon the shoulders of the powers and principalities. They must keep this world in good order. They will be judged by their failure to do so. The world would be in sorry shape without them. I discuss this at length in chapter 6.

To his set-apart people, however, God has given a different responsibility. He has made us responsible for embracing, displaying, and proclaiming his kingdom. The powers maintain an old order that is passing away. God's people must welcome the new order. On this side of the second coming, the new order does not take the shape of a territorial empire with provincial concerns. It is a transterritorial network of congregations whose life together bears witness to God's kingdom. Our responsibility does not change when we enjoy temporary success by worldly measures.

As ancient Israel's priests teach us (see chapter 22), God sometimes sets a group of people apart from wider society to carry out specific responsibilities that others are not able to do. To carry out their responsibilities (e.g., studying and teaching Torah, serving in the tabernacle, hosting cities of refuge), the priests could not participate in other activities that were essential to wider society's thriving (e.g., fighting wars, owning property, judging civil cases, leading tribes). The priests benefited greatly from the service of the other tribes and their leaders, but that did not make them responsible for doing what those rulers were responsible for doing. They were only responsible for what God had given them to do. It would have been irresponsible of them to neglect their responsibilities in

order to assume responsibility for economic, judicial, and political concerns that fell beyond their mandate. It would have been prideful of them
to assume that they could do everything well.

Nothing could be more clear in Scripture than that God has set his
people apart from all other people in this world to carry out a unique
function that ultimately serves the world's best interests. Both testaments
use priestly language to describe our unique set-apart status. We are
priests, part of a priestly kingdom and a holy nation (Exod 19:5–6; 1 Pet
2:4–5; Rev 1:5–6; 5:10; 20:6).

*13. What about human rights? Should Christians seek to make sure people's
rights are properly protected and respected?*

God has not appointed his people to police the world and "make
sure" of anything. To "make sure" of something requires force and the
sword. Scripture is quite clear that God has given the sword to the powers
and not to the church. Nonetheless, God's people should care about the
dignity of all people. This is why, from the very beginning, God called
his people, Israel, to treat all people with dignity, especially those whom
other nations tended to rob of their dignity. We must do so, first of all, by
giving full dignity to all people where we do have authority: within the
body of Christ. This will be a witness to those who are outside the body.
It testifies that a group of people can truly give dignity to all people in
this world.

Our witness will not be limited to body life. Wherever we go—work,
stores, schools—we should treat all people with equal dignity. In fact, we
acquire the skills to do so within the body of Christ so we can stand out
as bright lights outside of the body. If wider society is already on board
with human rights, then our witness won't stand out as much in this area.
In such cases, there are probably enough power bearers in play who are
pursuing equal rights. If wider society is not already on board with human rights, then our witness will stand out more. People will ask us to
give an account of our contrary practices and we must be eager to do so.
We must speak what we have learned to be true in God's kingdom. We
must encourage all who will listen to embrace this kingdom and learn
from God's wisdom and righteousness. We must invite them to join us
both within the body and alongside the body in honoring all life.

Should our skills be helpful to wider society, some of us may even
find employment in occupations that promote the dignity of all people in

a specific way. But the fundamental posture of the church must remain the same: *God's justice is a gift that we invite all people to embrace and not a law that we have been called to enforce.* We want people to receive God's gift as a gift, just like we did. We want it to be sincere and not calculated. We want it to remain gospel.

14. How should the church remain kingdom centered during challenging or pivotal times, like during the Nazi regime, the civil rights movement, or the displacement of refugees?

These scenarios are quite different and should be treated separately. Moreover, different churches find themselves positioned differently in relation to these diverse scenarios. For instance, there were churches in Germany who found themselves struggling to survive in a land that Hitler ruled. For them, being God's people meant maintaining a distinct identity from the governing structures so as not to serve Hitler's idolatrous ends. It meant continuing to embrace, display, and proclaim God's reign. God's kingdom principles remained their way of life even when society outlawed them.

Churches in similar situations today may have to maintain a somewhat low profile, as the early church did, if they hope to avoid needless persecution. Christians would have to pray fervently that God would bring the governing ideology crashing down upon itself whether from within or from the outside. They would have to trust God to use other powers, like surrounding nations, to bring down a wicked regime. Churches outside of that regime would want to maintain their witness to the kingdom as well. They would support struggling churches, host exiled believers who were forced to flee, and seek the Spirit's leading as to how they might carry out, in their time and place, what God's people were uniquely authorized and equipped to do.

As to the civil rights movement, the church's response is similar. We must grant equal status within the community before, during, and after wider society embraces the idea. We should also treat all people outside the body with equal dignity before, during, and after it is popular to do so. We are not responsible for forcing all people to do and believe as we do, but in word and deed we should convey our convictions and invite others into the kingdom that supports them.

As to refugees, the church's response is twofold. First, we would not assume that it is our responsibility to solve society's refugee problem.

It's not. We are not the powers whom God has appointed to maintain national borders. This land is not "our land" to manage. We are not privy to all information that would be essential for nations seeking to develop sound policy. We will not play God or covet governmental responsibility because we have a soft spot for refugees. We will have to trust God to oversee the powers and to make space for people. Sometimes the nation in which we live will be the best place for them; other times it will not. We should not assume that our nation is always best.

Second, to the extent that refugees find their way through the borders and into our towns, we will extend the same dignity to them as to everyone else. We will be especially eager to welcome believing refugees into our churches and, through them, to develop a vibrant witness to the wider refugee community. As Christians and heirs of Ancient Israel, we can relate to their displaced status. The Israelites spent much of their Old Testament existence as refugees, and Christians today should recognize with the Apostles Peter and Paul that our country is not our home (1 Pet 2:11; Phil 3:20). God's kingdom is our home and it transcends national borders. To us, displaced people are not political problems to be solved, but fellow refugees.

15. What about people like Mother Teresa who dedicated her life to the poor and less fortunate or Martin Luther King Jr. who worked tirelessly for the rights of African Americans?

People with radical devotion to specific causes have much to teach us. People like Mother Teresa who take vows of chastity and poverty are especially well-positioned to show us what a life of unhindered devotion to Christ can look like (1 Cor 7:32–35). Still, all individuals who would serve as a model of kingdom living would have to seek first God's kingdom, God's way. They would have to be active members of their church family. Their closest family and friends would be fellow kingdom seekers. They would have to embrace, display, and proclaim the kingdom in word and deed.

This is precisely what we find in people like Mother Teresa and Martin Luther King Jr. She was a devout Roman Catholic, and his witness grew out of his membership in the black Baptist Church. King's grounding in the church provided not only the support base for his agenda, but the criteria by which he carried out that agenda. He adamantly opposed violent forms of revolt because he was committed to the nonviolent way of Jesus. Christian social reformers who distance their work from the church and make no effort at a holistic witness to God's kingdom unhinge their work from the gospel. They may accomplish great things and the world may be better off because of them, but it won't be the specific task to which God has assigned his people. For Mother Teresa and King, that was certainly *not* the case.

Nonetheless, many people embraced the civil rights dimension of King's cause without his gospel framework. For many Americans today, the notion of equality is a civic virtue with no need for Jesus, the church, or God's kingdom. At some point—I'm not sure exactly when—this work went from being church-rooted kingdom witness to a good worldly cause. What began as kingdom mission eventually became conventional wisdom. Christians need not lament this. The majority culture may not have embraced the gospel, but it embraced a fruit of the gospel and is better off for it.

King's earliest proclamation still would have been faithful kingdom work had wider society never embraced it. We would have reason to celebrate his labor for the gospel had he never been chosen to represent a cause that went viral. His work bore witness to the kingdom not because it made inroads into the national psyche, but because there is neither black nor white in God's kingdom. So if one wants to embrace the kingdom legacy of King, one must embrace the church-grounded, full-gospel framework that enveloped his work. But if one wants to be a public advocate for a single kingdom virtue—divorced from the church's life and the wider kingdom framework—then one should not identify that work as "kingdom work," but as benevolent public service.

Striving to Remain Faithful

16. How do we as a church know if we are being faithful to God's mission? Are there certain litmus tests that reveal whether we are on the right track?

Scripture's teaching about God's kingdom is the most direct litmus test. I list numerous attributes of God's kingdom in chapter 11. A church that is committed to embracing, displaying, and proclaiming God's kingdom is on the right path. Of course, what it looks like to reflect God's kingdom in different times and places will change. This is why God gave us his Spirit. The Holy Spirit guides us as we face new circumstances that raise new questions (John 14:16–18; 16:12–14).

We should not burden ourselves with the fear of not getting it perfectly right. The kingdom is not a job that won't be completed if we don't complete it. It is a gift that we embrace and strive to faithfully display. Seldom do we perfectly display God's kingdom. Fortunately, God's purpose for us does not require perfection. If it did, he would not have chosen to make his appeal through us. There is something about our imperfections that enables us to offer God's gift as a gift that none of us deserve and for which all of us must be grateful (1 Cor 1:25—2:5).

Though the kingdom's coming does not depend on us, people's opportunity to receive it does. The Apostle Paul reminds us that lost people's ability to hear and embrace the message of salvation depends on God's people proclaiming it to them (Rom 10:13–15). Although God is pleased to extend his offer through imperfect vessels, he has little use for inactive and unfruitful vessels (Matt 25:14–30; John 15:1–2). So while we may not do so perfectly, we must bear witness to God's kingdom continuously.

17. How do we sustain a kingdom-centered church life?

First and foremost, the gospel must be taught regularly. One way or another, the kingdom vision must remain at the forefront of the body's mind and life. Is it taught to potential members? Is it integral to the congregation's worship services? Is it revisited regularly enough that it remains on the forefront of people's minds? The church of which I am part revisits the church's nature and mission each year at our annual retreat. The big picture Bible story must also be taught. Most teaching focuses on small snippets of Scripture, but the gospel is best grasped in light of the overarching story. The kingdom vision is counterintuitive enough that people must remain in the world of Scripture. Otherwise, the steady stream of this world's stories will drown it out.

In addition, the members of the body must fervently love one another. To truly love one another, they must know one another. They must be involved in each other's lives enough to know when someone is suffering or in need. Eating meals together makes a big difference. Serving together also helps. Sharing possessions goes a long way, as does living in close proximity. Distance inhibits all practices that make for deep interpersonal relationships. Small groups are key. In large congregations it is easy for people to get lost in the crowd. Where size is too large for all members to know each other intimately, small group participation should be integral to membership. Better yet, why not require it of members?

Such small groups should avoid becoming mere affinity groups. They should be kingdom cells or microcosms of God's reign, which include people of all ages, ethnicities, professions, and marital statuses.

Fraternal admonition is another central practice. As people drift from their kingdom calling, fellow believers ought to lovingly correct and redirect them. The kingdoms of this world are deeply appealing and alluring. Repentance is a vital practice—not just individual repentance, but institutional repentance. Sometimes the whole body goes off course and only a corporate corrective can get everyone back on track.

A strong vision of the priesthood of all believers is also key. If we are to grow into the full stature of Christ, leaders must equip the saints for the work of ministry and not do ministry on behalf of the saints (Eph 4:11–16). All members must do their part because that is what God's kingdom is like and we have been called to reflect the kingdom. Many churches have members who don't think their regular service is essential to congregational thriving. This lie is never taught overtly. It is simply deduced from the fact that the body seems to do just fine even when members check out for months at a time. Sometimes no one even contacts an absent member while they are gone. When we do, we usually communicate that their presence at gatherings is missed. We should communicate—because it should be true—that we are hurting without them because their unique gifts are sorely missed.

18. How should Christians position themselves to be visible demonstrations of God's kingdom before the world's eyes?

We are already visible in this world. We are visible in our neighborhoods. We are visible in our jobs. People see us in the marketplace. The question is, when people look at us, *what do they see?* Do they see us as solitary individuals like them, scraping to cope or get by? Or do they see us as members of a joy-filled, tightly knit community? Do they see us loving one another? Are the members of our church a part of our lives in such a way that they often come up in our conversations? Do they hear us proclaiming the kingdom?

The Great Commission puts it best: "As you are going, make disciples" (Matt 28:19–20). God has not called us to a new set of otherworldly or superhuman activities. He has called us to inhabit this world in ways that reflect his kingdom. So we must raise our children with a kingdom-first mind-set, care for our property with a kingdom-first mind-set, and carry out our work with a kingdom-first mind-set. We must do all that we do for the glory of God (1 Pet 4:11), and we must not do it alone. We should do it together in such a way that people can see that followers of Jesus no longer view people from a human point of view. The church already has an infinite number of connection points with lost people in this world. We don't need any more until we make the most of the ones we already have.

19. What does a kingdom-centered approach mean for living in solidarity with the poor or disenfranchised?

Living in solidarity with the poor and disenfranchised should never be disconnected from the gospel message. This means that it should not be ignored *and* that it should not be patterned after models of solidarity that are not grounded in the gospel. The good news is not that poverty is ending because the poor of this world have a new, more dedicated group of benefactors. The good news is that God's kingdom is breaking in and that communities who embrace kingdom economics are spreading throughout all cities and nations. The economic vision of God's kingdom entails that no member of the believing community goes without food, clothing, and shelter. So every member of every congregation must stand in solidarity with the poorest members of their body.

When members of Christ's body share with one another, they are blessed by God and there is usually enough to go around for everyone. When communities live like this, the poor and disenfranchised outside the body will want to be a part of it and should be enthusiastically welcomed into it. In contexts where wealth is readily available, the abundance will be spread around, and the poor will be provided for and lifted up. Where scarcity is rampant throughout society and the church, members will share in one another's poverty. They will help one another out in tangible ways that ease the burden of poverty. Their joy in fellowship and witness will give meaning and direction to life. It will give them the kind of prosperity that money cannot buy.

As part of a global fellowship, Christian solidarity will not end there. Congregations in dire straits need not suffer absolute impoverishment even while their particular region struggles financially. They may call upon congregations who are thriving in distant regions to stand in solidarity with them. When the Apostle Paul learned that believers in Jerusalem were struggling financially, he solicited help from congregations in Greece who were much better off (2 Cor 8–9). Part of the good news is that God has incorporated us all into a global fellowship. Wealthy churches should find ways to empower the witness of churches in the poorest cities of this world.

20. How do kingdom-centered congregations avoid becoming insular?

For starters, we should learn from and partner with others churches. No church should exist in isolation. Many are part of specific Christian traditions that bind them to a wide web of congregations. Yet even those from independent congregational backgrounds remain part of the global network of Christ's church. So it is important to identify sister churches who are striving to cultivate kingdom values in creative ways. The creative practices of other congregations can often ignite the imagination of our own. The congregation of which I am a part deliberately participates in joint retreats with other congregations in order to foster opportunities for cross pollination.

Churches may also participate in interdenominational conferences that are dedicated to forming and sustaining congregations with kingdom sensibilities. The Ekklesia Project, for instance, hosts an annual gathering that focuses on the gospel's radical demands for congregational life. Its goal is to "foster conversation about the Church among theologians, pastors and congregations."[1] We must avoid the notion that only our paid staff or appointed leaders should attend such gatherings. The more members of a body participate, the more we will learn and grow together.

Many churches have also found it extremely helpful to visit congregations in cultures quite different from their own. Affluent believers usually find it convicting to visit churches in poorer countries. Yet too often the lessons we learn focus on personal wealth and generosity. We also have much to learn about congregational life. Poorer congregations often excel in communal solidarity, economic sharing, and unapologetic gospel proclamation. Congregations often send individuals, typically youth, on short-term trips to somehow bless poorer nations. We may also see short-term trips as opportunities for groups of adult church members to learn from congregations in poorer nations. They have much to teach us about kingdom living.

1. http://www.ekklesiaproject.org/.

Index of Names and Subjects

Index of Biblical References